The SQUIRE

The SQUIRE

A Life of George Alexander Baird
Gentleman Rider 1861 – 1893

Richard Onslow

Harrap　London

First published in Great Britain 1980
by GEORGE G. HARRAP & CO. LTD
182 High Holborn, London WC1V 7AX

© *Richard Onslow* 1980

ISBN 0 245 53612 4

Designed by Robert Wheeler

Filmset by Woolaston Parker Ltd, Leicester
Printed and bound in Great Britain by
Redwood Burn Ltd, Trowbridge and Esher

CONTENTS

ILLUSTRATIONS

ACKNOWLEDGMENTS

In collecting material for a biography of George Alexander Baird, the Squire, I have had cause to be extremely grateful to many people who, out of the kindness of their hearts, have gone to the trouble of helping me. In particular I owe a large debt to Mr David E. Baird of Newburgh, Fife. Mr Baird is the son of the Squire's first cousin, the late Brigadier-General E. W. D. Baird, and has been good enough to furnish me with invaluable information about the background of the Squire, his early life and other matters.

To my publisher Mr Paull Harrap as well as to Mr Peter O'Sullevan I am deeply indebted for their invaluable criticism of my first draft of this book. I have also to acknowledge my gratitude to Mr Tony Sweeney for permission to reproduce his picture of The Rejected, on whom the Squire won thirteen races. The rider of The Rejected in this picture is almost certainly the Squire.

I am grateful to Mr L. F. Bell, Editorial Director of the *Sporting Chronicle*, for providing me with copies of his paper's obituary of the Squire and reports concerning the circumstances of his death. Similarly, I am greatly obliged to the Editor of the *Glasgow Herald* for sending me a copy of the obituary carried by his paper.

To Colonel Peter Hamer, Secretary to the Stewards of the Jockey Club, I am exceedingly grateful for access to information about the Squire that is only to be found in the minutes of the club.

I must express my thanks to Mr Patrick Strong, Keeper of the Eton College Library, and Miss E. S. Leedham-Green, Assistant Keeper of the Archives at Cambridge University, for the necessarily scant information of what may euphemistically be called the Squire's education.

I should like further to thank Mr David Hedges for details of the dispersal sale of the Squire's horses at Tattersalls; Mr John Marquis, London Sports Editor of Thomson Regional Newspapers, for guidance through what seemed to me the arid area of boxing literature; the President and members of the Whittington Barracks Golf Club for allowing me access to their club house, formerly the grandstand of Lichfield racecourse; Mr W. J. Ennion, the well-known Newmarket solicitor, who gave me some very useful background information about the Newmarket district; and our local Windlesham solicitor, Mr John

Hill, who obtained a copy of the Squire's will on my behalf and interpreted the legal jargon.

I should like to acknowledge the debt I owe the retired Newmarket trainer, Mr Sam Armstrong, who passed on his father's impression of the Squire to me.

To Mrs Sarah Clapton, I offer my thanks for the care with which she typed this book. Her own considerable knowledge of racing, her skill and her patience all stood her in good stead.

Finally, I must acknowledge all the help I have received from my wife, Barbara, who has endured endless hours of proof-reading uncomplainingly.

December 1979   RICHARD ONSLOW

1 RECIPE FOR A RENEGADE

WHEN he was no more than eight years of age, George Alexander Baird inherited a fortune of two million pounds on the death of his father in 1870, and, six years later, another of about half as much from an uncle.

Having decided to devote the best part of his immense resources of wealth and youthful energy to horse racing, he made a singularly inauspicious start by getting himself warned off the Turf before he had even come of age. On being reinstated, he owned a Derby winner while still only twenty-five and developed into a remarkably accomplished amateur jockey. In a single season he was to ride more than sixty winners on the flat, a feat that the vast majority of professionals have never been able to even hope to accomplish.

In a love-life that was no less dramatic than his racing career, for all that he was more often drunk than sober for weeks on end, he succeeded the heir to the throne as the recipient of the favours of the most celebrated beauty of the day. He abducted a marchioness and frequently gratified his desires in some distinctly unrarified atmospheres. He spent many thousands of pounds as a patron of prize-fighting and otherwise found his amusement in heavy betting, cock-fighting, dog-fighting, brawling and any other pursuit that made a noise, all of which may seem hardly edifying for a product of Eton and Cambridge.

Eventually, on the other side of the world, he died, worn out by the pace of his profligacy, at the age of thirty-one. Like an erratic comet, the young Scottish millionaire had scorched his path across the Turf until burning himself out long before due season.

Convention and the social niceties he defied all his life. For the law of the land he had a grudging respect, which rarely prevented him from breaking it, especially those acts relating to the maintaining of the Queen's Peace, it being his custom to pay one of his legion of parasites to play the part of whipping-boy by taking the rap whenever the constabulary should intervene.

For the rules and ordinances of the Jockey Club he had a profound contempt, and he flouted them, though not always with impunity, every day of his adult life, his continual breach of them being the keeping of horses in other people's names. In the youthful arrogance of his millions, tempered by hardly a jot of worldly wisdom and never steadied by the counsels of his elders, he set himself at variance with man and nature, and though man afforded him much merriment for a while, nature was not long in exacting her price.

George Alexander Baird belonged to a family that came to the forefront of the commercial, political and sporting life in Scotland through the diligence and foresight of its members during the years of the Industrial Revolution. The founder of the family's fortunes had been Alexander Baird, who was born in 1765, five years after King George III had come to the throne.

Originally a farmer in a small way, Alexander Baird had lived in abject poverty while he struggled to earn enough to keep his wife and their seven sons. When the local minister complained about the wind whistling through the doors and windows of the manse, one of the Baird boys capped the ecclesiastical tale of woe with the observation that the holes and fissures in the walls of their house were so large that the cats and dogs came through them.

Eventually Alexander Baird freed himself from the misery of trying to make a living from the land when he and his seven sons, William, John, James, Robert, Douglas, George and David, became miners. At first they dug for coal, and then, recognizing the shape of things to come as industrialization increased, for iron. The short railway line between Monkland and Kirkintilloch, the first in Scotland, had been laid as early as 1826, and soon a whole network was under construction to meet the needs of the Glasgow area. As more and more track was laid, the demand for iron became insatiable and the seven Baird brothers worked almost all the hours of the day to meet it. Later, having put a bit of capital together, they were able to undertake contracts for whole lines, but instead of money, they took shares in the railway companies by way of payment, thereby laying the foundation of their great wealth and that of their own sons.

In 1826, the year of the opening of the Monkland to Kirkintilloch line, the brothers took a lease on the coalfields at Sunnyside, Hollandhirst and New Gartsherrie. Two years later, they extended their interests to the ironstone in the lands of Cairnhill. Then, in 1830, the year of the death of George IV, James Baird, at the early age of twenty-eight, assumed the management of a family business that, though flourishing, was still a long way from the height of its fortunes. Alexander Baird, the patriarch, died three years later in 1833, and by the middle of the century the heirs of the once penniless farmer controlled ironworks and collieries in Ayr, Stirling, Dunbarton and south of the border in Cumberland, so that William Baird & Co., the firm founded by the seven brothers, was in the forefront in the industrialization of western Scotland.

Having made their money from coal and iron, the Baird brothers invested some of it in making themselves landed gentry and entered public life. James acquired the Auchmelden estate in Aberdeenshire, served as Member of Parliament for Falkirk Burghs from 1851 until 1857 and was also Deputy Lieutenant for the counties of Ayr and Inverness. A deeply religious man, James Baird gave no less than £200,000 to the Church of Scotland, thereby provoking the jibe about it being the highest insurance premium against fire ever paid. The bulk of his fortune, however, went in a very different direction, as, little dreaming of the use to which it would be put, he left it to his nephew George Alexander at his death in 1876.

William, who made his home at Elie in Fife, was also a Member of Parliament. George, who married Cecilia, daughter of Admiral Hatton of Clonard, in London on 15th November 1858, bought the 18,000 acres of the Strichen estate from the 14th Lord Lovat in 1855, while David paid £150,000 for the Stichil property a few miles north of Kelso in Roxburghshire, and, dying while still only forty-four in 1860, bequeathed it to his brother George.

Like his elder brother James, George Baird was of a distinctly religious turn of mind, making up with his zeal for what he lacked in formal education in the scriptures. His passion for building churches earned the derision of James Merry, another Glaswegian ironmaster, whose mean and suspicious nature belied his name. The story goes, though it is probably apocryphal, that Merry bet George Baird £5 that he did not even know the Lord's Prayer. Upon Baird beginning, 'I believe in . . .' Merry stopped him straightaway and paid up, saying, 'Hoots! I never thought ye'd ha' known it, mon.'

George Alexander, the only son of George and Cecilia Baird, was born at 10 Queen Street, Edinburgh, on 30th September 1861, just seventy-five days before the death of the Prince Consort. There is an element of irony about one of those completely contrasting individuals having made his entry into this world just as the other was about to take his leave of it. The Prince Consort, with a deep sense of purpose, had always sought to raise the moral and intellectual tone of the country, whereas George Baird, without any conscious purpose at all, was to do all he could to lower it.

The first and greatest disaster in the life of George Baird came with the death of his father in 1870. In consequence he was deprived of paternal guidance and control in the formative years of adolescence and early manhood when he desperately needed to learn the virtues of moderation, thrift and self-restraint, and to acquire judgment, before his inheritance freed him from all the discipline to which the vast majority of mankind is subject.

The loss of a father is sad for any boy, but for one of George Baird's character and expectations it can be, as it was in his case, a blow from which there is no recovery. By that time all his uncles were either also dead or too old to have helped in bringing him up, even if his mother had been agreeable to their doing so. Instead of having a proper preparation for the responsibilities of wealth, George Baird grew up in the care of a doting mother who readily indulged the most ridiculous of his childish whims while the formation of his mind and character was completely neglected. Rather than ensure that he acquired some rudiments of education, taste and culture from tutors before embarking upon his formal education, Cecilia Baird allowed her adored son to do as he pleased, roaming and riding the countryside around Stichil, which, though lacking the magnificence of palaces like Floors and Drumlanrigg, was one of the finest houses in the south of Scotland. It was demolished in the early 1930s.

While George Baird ran riot, unsupervised and unchecked, during the three or four years following the death of his father, his mother was finding the problems of widowhood far greater than might be supposed. Contrary to what was ever to be the case with his son, the elder George Baird had a highly developed sense of the value of money, having had to work extremely hard for very little as a young man, and an abhorrence of its being wasted. Accordingly, he had left his fortune so that it was under the control of trustees during the minority of his son, and so tightly tied up that Cecilia Baird had scarcely sufficient funds for the maintenance of Stichil, let alone meeting other demands which steadily increased as George grew older and ever more extravagant. Those trustees, appointed under the will of his father, were reluctant to make available any more of the money under their control than was absolutely necessary. In consequence, Cecilia Baird was always on the worst terms with those who were supposed to be the guardians of her son's interests and became engaged in a running battle that reached its ridiculous climax in a court action to secure an increase in the allowance they made to her. The absurdity of the situation did not go unnoticed and was the subject of an anonymous skit.

When sent to Eton for the start of the Michaelmas half of 1874, a few days before his thirteenth birthday, George Baird was inevitably lacking the most superficial good manners, let alone any incipient sophistication. Hopes of his achieving even the most modest academic distinction cannot have been high in those who bore the principal responsibility for his education: namely, Mr T. J. P. Carter, his housemaster, and the Rev. J. H. Merriott. The Rev. Merriott had joined the staff at the outset of the same half, and having survived the early ordeal of trying to make a classical scholar of the wilful youth from the Border, continued to teach at Eton until 1896.

There never was any prospect of George Baird being a success at Eton. Unamenable to discipline or living in an organized community, he never displayed the slightest aptitude for academic work, nor any promise of prowess at sport. Unaccustomed to the give and take of life, he soon found that he could not have his own way all the time with his schoolfellows as he did with the ghillies and grooms at home at Stichil, and reacted by flying into fits of ungovernable temper. All his contemporaries could remember of him during his short time at Eton were those tantrums in which he would indulge in such acts of senseless destruction as stamping on a valuable gold watch and grinding it to pieces beneath his heel. Notwithstanding such unprepossessing behaviour, he was able to become disenchanted with Eton before Eton became disenchanted with him. Having ungraciously declared, 'I don't like the place,' he left at the end of the Michaelmas half of 1875.

Returning to Stichil, he seems to have spent most of the next four years there under the hopelessly inadequate supervision of his mother. As a memento of his boyhood she had Robert Frain paint a portrait of him mounted on a pony. This was hung over the mantelpiece of one of the principal reception rooms at Stichil. The artist's chalk sketch for it was still adorning the wall of the near-by village school at the time of its subject's death nearly twenty years later.

A final attempt to inculcate a modicum of culture into George Baird was made by sending him to Cambridge. In November 1879, he went through the formalities of entry into Magdalene College, of which he is listed as a pensioner for the years 1880 and 1881.

What George Baird did acquire at Cambridge was the love of riding fast horses which was soon to become the ruling passion of his life. Magdalene, in those days, enjoyed a great reputation as a sporting college at which undergraduates could do pretty much as they liked, attendance at lectures being no more than an optional addition to all the amusements available to a lot of rich young men.

George Baird was able to take full advantage of the freedom afforded by this congenial atmosphere. Having raised the necessary funds, either by way of a loan or through the uncharacteristic cooperation of his trustees, he acquired a huge stable of hunters so that he was always better mounted than almost any other follower of the Cambridge Drag.

The drag ran over a large area of country on all sides of the city, with Newmarket, just fourteen miles away, being well within the radius of its pack. Whenever the drag fetched up at Newmarket, several of the trainers and other members of the racing community would join in. Thus many a rich undergraduate was able to widen his knowledge of the world of sport by making his first, tentative contact with the Turf, while more than one Newmarket trainer made the valuable acquaintanceship of a young man who was soon to embark upon the ownership of racehorses on a considerable scale. George Baird was one of many for whom the road from Cambridge has led to Newmarket, where surreptitious attendance at meetings has left an ineradicable taste for the Turf.

Quite possibly he already had a vague predilection for racing from his background. As has already been mentioned, his family had a close association, though hardly the friendship, with their fellow Glaswegian ironmaster James Merry, who had died in 1877. Merry had won the Derby with Thormanby in 1860, and again with Doncaster in 1873, while Mat Dawson, Jimmy Waugh and then Bob Peck had trained for

LEFT: *James Baird gave a fortune to the Church of Scotland and left another (which was used for a very different purpose) to his nephew, the Squire* MARY EVANS PICTURE LIBRARY

CENTRE: *the Squire's pious father, George Baird* EDINBURGH CITY LIBRARIES

RIGHT: *the Squire's first cousin, Brigadier-General E. W. D. Baird, who gained distinction as soldier and sportsman*

BELOW: *Stichil House, built by the Squire's father, George Baird, in pure Scottish baronial style after he had demolished the old house on inheriting the property from his brother David in 1860. This new building was in turn pulled down in about 1930* EDINBURGH CITY LIBRARIES

ABOVE: *Bedford Lodge, Newmarket — the stables are to the right — in the days when the Squire played host to some singularly unselect company*

LEFT: *Newmarket's Greyhound Inn — long demolished — where the Squire made his fateful acquaintance with the fighting fraternity*

ABOVE RIGHT: *Newmarket High Street at the time when the Squire's 'goings-on' at Bedford Lodge were one of the prime subjects of its gossip*

RIGHT: *Dog-fighting* (MARY EVANS PICTURE LIBRARY) *and cock-fighting* (BBC HULTON PICTURE LIBRARY) *— both made illegal earlier in the century — were a source of much pleasure to the Squire*

LEFT: *Puritanical little Martin Gurry — the first of the Squire's private trainers — who took a poor view of his employer and a still poorer one of his friends*

RIGHT: *the third and last of the Squire's private trainers, easy-going Joe Cannon*

CENTRE: *the long-suffering Charlie Morton in later life. He was private trainer to the Squire at Bedford Lodge from 1888 to 1892*

BELOW: *the Stevens family with whom the Squire had a great many horses in training at Compton in Berkshire*

him in his large private stable at Russley Park, a few miles from Lambourn.

In 1859, James Merry had been elected Member of Parliament for Falkirk Burghs and had kept his seat, despite a petition to deprive him of it by his unsuccessful opponent – George Alexander Baird's father. Some time later, Merry was called upon to answer to his constituents, all true sons of the Kirk, for running a horse in France on the 'Sawbeth' day. Legend has it that Merry outfaced his accusers by saying, 'I won the Frenchman's money and I brought it back to spend in auld Scotland.'

Although he did nothing but run as wild as the Border country itself during his boyhood at Stichil, it seems probable that George Baird heard of the triumphs of Doncaster, of Marie Stuart, who won the Oaks and St Leger in the same year, and of other horses belonging to his disagreeable old compatriot.

Another factor in encouraging George Baird's enthusiasm for the Turf could have been the example of his cousin Douglas, who was five years his senior and the son of William Baird, who had given his name to the family firm. Douglas Baird displayed an early interest in racing and was still a young man when becoming a patron of Jimmy Ryan's Green Lodge stable at Newmarket. Jimmy Ryan, who had been born at Gullane in 1836, was yet another Lowland Scot to play a part on the late Victorian racing scene. On becoming too heavy to carry on riding as a steeplechase jockey, he had trained at Irvine for the seven years until 1871, when he went to Newmarket. There he married Rosa Jarvis, sister of the Waterwitch House trainer Bill Jarvis and great-aunt of the former Newmarket trainer, Ryan Jarvis, who bears Rosa's husband's name. In due course, Jimmy Ryan would give George Baird the leg up on to a horse that had won a classic, one of the very few of such distinction ever to have been ridden by an amateur in public.

It is unlikely that George Baird ever attended a single lecture during the two years that he was at Cambridge, and if he did, he would not have understood a word of it. There was therefore no question of his sitting any preliminary examination, let alone taking a degree.

Hence, when he came down from Cambridge, George Baird was not only still uneducated but quite unsophisticated, and so far from being wise in the ways of the world as to be easy prey for the flatcatchers – 'flat', in contradistinction to its musical antonym 'sharp', being the prevailing slang for a greenhorn or gullible innocent. These flatcatchers, who were to be found all over the West End of London, were young men of good family with incomes of the same meagre proportions as their taste for work, professional gamblers with unsavoury reputations, and ex-jockeys whose dishonesty was more their downfall than incompetence, together with other racecourse riff-raff and prize-fighters who preferred to earn a living as hired thugs rather than by putting on gloves in the ring. All these odious, obnoxious and obsequious individuals, and anyone with a horse to sell or a bawdy tale to tell, rode high in the favour of George Baird as they waited for him to come into absolute control of his millions.

They called him the Squire. Ever since the term ceased to have any armorial or territorial significance, Englishmen have addressed as 'Squire' those to whom they wish to show respect when none is due.

2 WARNED OFF

THE Squire could scarcely have found a less propitious time at which to make his début on to the Turf. Racing was only just beginning to live down the unsavoury reputation that it had earned in the middle of the century, but memories persisted of how the Marquess of Hastings had squandered a fortune betting at Newmarket, Ascot and Epsom, while many of the smaller courses had been little better than thieves' kitchens with equine sideshows in the 1860s. Riots, like that in which the grandstand was showered with bricks at Shrewsbury in 1874, were not uncommon, and both at the provincial meetings and those in the suburbs of London, the welshers, so long the bane of racing, and the musclemen who protected them, ensured that there was precious little sport or pleasure to be had.

As a consequence, therefore, of the heavy plungers like Lord Hastings, on the one hand, and notorious welshers like 'Big' Fisher, against whom stewards and police seemed powerless, on the other, rich and poor alike had come to look upon racing with considerable distaste, despite all that Admiral Rous had tried to do to weed out the vicious and villainous elements. The first important turning in the road came in 1876 when the Jockey Club raised the minimum value of plates and sweepstakes from £50 to £100, thereby enforcing the closure of a number of disreputable suburban courses like West Drayton, Kingsbury, Navestock and Bromley through their inability to find the necessary prize money. Three years later, Parliament reinforced the Jockey Club's action with the passing of

Anderson's Metropolitan Racecourses Bill, which prohibited the holding of any race meeting within fifteen miles of the centre of London. Because of all the scandals in the past and the fears for the future to which they gave rise, the Jockey Club and the rest of racing's establishment were more than mildly apprehensive about a young man of George Baird's impulsiveness unleashing his millions on the Turf.

Registering his colours as the eye-shattering combination of cardinal jacket and Cambridge Blue cap, the Squire began racing with a few hunter 'chasers in the North in 1880. Even ownership on that modest scale created considerable difficulties for him at that time, as his Glaswegian trustees were proving even more parsimonious in his case than they were in that of his mother. He would not come of age until 30th September 1882, and meanwhile had to have recourse to any stratagem that he, or, as was generally the case, his friends, could devise in order to raise money for his racing and a lot of other less laudable self-indulgences.

Once, confiding his urgent need of £5,000 to a friend, the Squire received an encouraging assurance that arrangements for this might be made. Thereupon the Squire promised the friend £500 if he were successful in effecting them, and was asked for an open cheque for that amount then and there. 'But I have no money at Coutts's,' protested the Squire.

'You soon will have,' replied his friend confidently. Next morning the latter took the first train to Glasgow, where he persuaded the trustees to lend the Squire £5,000 from the funds they held, to be repaid at a fair rate of interest from the allowance made to him, rather than let him go to the 'Sixty Per Schenters', the notorious London moneylenders. The trustees agreed to wire authorization of the money to Coutts's branch in the Strand, with the result that the conductor of these negotiations was outside its doors before they opened the following morning, and long before the Squire could learn of the dramatic improvement in his balance, to cash that open cheque for £500. Thus did the Squire pay £500 for lending himself his own money.

Rightly assuming that the trustees would be horrified at his owning racehorses, the Squire spared them the sorrow of such knowledge by using the name of 'Mr Abington' for the purposes of racing, Abington being one of the properties that he owned in Scotland. Contrary to what is the case today, when Rule 40 states, 'No owner shall make use of an assumed name,' it was recognized practice in the last century, as the then Rule 21 provided for the registration of an assumed name for an annual fee of £25, provided an owner did not use more than one such name, nor his own while the registration was in effect. Even after he had come of age, and right up to the end of his life, the Squire continued both to run his horses and to ride in the name of 'Mr Abington'. Only in the *General Stud Book* are his broodmares recorded as being the property of Mr G. A. Baird.

One of the first horses to carry the cardinal jacket and Cambridge Blue cap with any degree of distinction was Alwina, who won races under National Hunt rules at Ayr, Lanark, Hawick and Langholm in 1880. In that year and the one following, the Squire also obtained considerable success with his hunters at the small meetings in the Border country and the North of England. For instance, he owned and rode the winners of three of the four races at Billingham on 30th May 1881, taking the Teesside Hurdle and the Billingham Tradesmen's Plate for hunters on Uncle Sam and the Tibbersley Hunters' Plate on Benvoglio II. That was the only occasion on which Billingham races were ever held. When the Stockton meeting had been transferred from Tibbersley to Mandale, Mr W. Caygale, who farmed the former area, tried to continue the original fixture as Billingham races, but the fields were too poor to make it a success.

Among the first friends the Squire made while going the rounds of the small country meetings during the year or two after he had come down from Cambridge was Bob Adams. A member of a famous Yorkshire racing family, Bob Adams trained at Hambleton in the hills above Thirsk in the North Riding.

The Squire also won races on the flat during 1881. With Denzil, a brown colt by the 1875 Derby winner Galopin, he won at Thirsk, Newcastle, Morpeth, Redcar and Newton, and with Beatrice a seller at York. Both those horses were probably trained for him by Adams. In all he won seventeen races that year.

By the early months of 1882 the Square was riding regularly in hunters' flat races, and occasionally over hurdles, in the South and Midlands. By far the most important of his achievements during that period was the winning of the big hurdle race at Kempton Park on Theophrastus, narrowly beating the mount of Arthur Nightingall, one of the greatest jump jockeys of all time. As the Squire was reported to have had £2,000 on Theophrastus, his financial difficulties must have been alleviated for a while.

The most regretable result of the Squire moving south as the time of his entering into his inheritance drew closer was his exchanging the guidance of the North Country horsemasters like Bob Adams for that of the lounge lizards of London. To those gentry, the principal attraction of racing was the opportunities it offered for making money without working. The more nefarious and underhand the means by which this was done, the cleverer they thought themselves, always mistaking dishonesty for shrewdness. They told the Squire that the manly rider was the rough rider, or, even worse, the dirty rider, who showed his contempt for rules and rivals alike, even, if occasion necessitated, by putting another man over the rails. By such methods, they told the impressionable youth of twenty, he could make himself as much respected by the other Gentleman Riders as the great Archer was by the youngest apprentice. And the Squire believed all that they told him.

His increasingly aggressive riding was noted by stewards at National Hunt meetings all over the country, and as his tactics deteriorated from being distinctly questionable, the feeling grew among both his regular rivals and those responsible for seeing fair play that 'Mr Abington' would have to be taught a lesson. Meanwhile he was making enemies and laying up trouble for himself in yet another way. A born philanderer, to whom the carnal aspects of love were a great deal more important than the romantic, he made advances in the crude, unsubtle way he had, to young girls and married women indiscriminately. In consequence, husbands, fathers, brothers and sweethearts fast accumulated scores to be settled with young Mr George Baird. As many of those gentlemen were stewards at the meetings where his riding was giving ever greater offence, retribution became inevitable.

Matters came to a head at the Easter meeting at Birmingham's Four Oaks Park course on 11th April 1882, when the Squire rode his own horse Billy Banks in the Hunters' Selling Flat Race. Although drifting from 6/4 to 4/1, Billy Banks won well enough, beating Master John, ridden by Mr E. P. Wilson, by eight lengths, only to be disqualified for having carried the wrong weight. More serious, though, than that successful technical objection by the Clerk of the Scales, was the complaint from Lord Harrington, who had finished last on Gartmore. He alleged that the Squire had not only made some highly offensive remarks about his competence as a rider, but had threatened to put him over the rails if he brought his mount too close to Billy Banks. On being confronted by the injured party after their return to the paddock, the best amends that the Squire could bring himself to make was to mutter rather sulkily, 'Beg pardon, I thought you were a bloody farmer.'

At the age of thirty-four, Lord Harrington, who had succeeded his father as 8th Earl the previous year, was an experienced race rider. Had he been offered a more contrite apology, all might have been well. As it was, he thought the offence done him by the presumptious youth compounded by the offhand, almost insolent apology, and reported the incident to the stewards of the meeting. The panel of stewards for National Hunt racing at Four Oaks Park consisted of the Duke of Rutland, the Duke of Montrose, the Duke of Hamilton, the Duke of Beaufort, the Earl of Bradford, Lord de Clifford, Viscount Cole, Sir William Throckmorton, the Hon. Cecil Howard, Mr G. E. Paget, Mr E. C. Ker Seymer and Mr W. E. Oakley. Not one of those men had any liking for the Squire, and at least two are known to have had grudges against him arising from his dalliance with their womenfolk. In the circumstances, it was impossible that the Squire should have had a fair hearing, and it must have been with no small satisfaction that whichever of the stewards were acting that day reported the case to the National Hunt Committee. As the stewards of the National Hunt Committee were also waiting for the opportunity to bring the Squire to book, it is far from certain that he was treated impartially by them either, for, although his offence was threatening to put another rider over the rails rather than having done so, he was warned off for two years. The punishment was a severe one, but the fact of its being for a stipulated period rather than *sine die* suggests that the object of it was, in fact, reformation rather than revenge.

When the stewards of the Jockey Club extended the sentence to meetings under their jurisdiction, the following notice appeared in the *Racing Calendar* of 24th April 1882:

Mr Abington (Mr G. A. Baird) having been reported by the Stewards of the Four Oaks Park Easter Meeting for foul riding in the Hunters' Selling Flat Race Plate . . . the Stewards of the Grand National Hunt Committee have decided that he be warned off every course where the Grand National Hunt Rules are in force, for two years from this date, and that during that period no horse his property, nominated by him, trained by him, or in any way under his care, joint care, management, or superintendance, be allowed to run for any race at any meeting where the Grand National Hunt Rules are in force; they further directed that the case be reported to the Stewards of the Jockey Club, who extended the sentence to all meetings under their rules.

Being declared a disqualified person was a heavy blow to the Squire.

Having found something he could do well, riding racehorses and winning on them had become the very essence of life for the young man who had proved a failure at Eton and Cambridge and graduated to almost complete rejection by society because of his uncouthness and pronounced preference for low company. Rather than sell off his horses in self-righteous high dudgeon, with some declaration to the effect that he would never be seen on a racecourse again, as many another man might have done, the Squire put them into the nominal ownership of Ross Smith, his most intimate friend at that time.

A tall, slim, prepossessing man, 'Stiffy' Smith came from an old Scottish family whose otherwise respectable reputation he did absolutely nothing to enhance. It was commonly estimated that this charming and plausible rogue wheedled more money out of the Squire than any of the other members of a highly competitive field. Charles Morton, who was to train for the Squire, went so far as to assert that he made more than the rest put together.

Having made arrangements for the disposition of his horses, the Squire decided to taste the legendary pleasures of Paris, where life had long been back to normal after the horrors of the siege that had ended the Franco-Prussian war twelve years earlier. International cooperation in racing was then in its infancy. Although the stewards of the French Jockey Club and the President of the American Jockey Club were already *ex officio* members of the Jockey Club, miscreants were yet to feel the full force of reciprocal agreements, so the Squire was free to enjoy the racing in France during his enforced retirement from the English Turf.

Six months after he had been warned off, the Squire came of age and was at long last freed from the heavy financial fetters with which his trustees had kept him in some sort of check during adolescence. In addition to almost £3,000,000-worth of investments in Scottish railways and other commercial undertakings, he entered into possession of three quarters of a million in ready money that had accumulated during his minority and vast estates in Scotland, which, together with the investments, brought in an income of £100,000 a year. Among his Scottish properties, some of which he never even visited, were the 18,000 acres of the Strichen estate in Aberdeenshire, those at Auchmelden in the same county, Kilmuir and Kingsburgh, which together extended to 50,000 acres in Inverness-shire, and Stichil House with all the land around it in Roxburghshire.

Although free from those grim and forbidding trustees, and the possessor of an income so large as to be almost incomprehensible when expressed in present-day values, the Squire was not complete master of that princely inheritance. His father, with a sense of family unity natural to a generation that had toiled long and hard together, had tied up the capital and property in strict entail. This made the Squire tenant for life, giving him the income and the next generation of the family, whether his own children or those of his cousins, a reversionary interest in the capital. The law of entail in Scotland being rather more flexible than that in England made the breaking of it a relatively straightforward matter, something of which the Squire was quick to take advantage. Having paid some £40,000 in compensation to the intended beneficiaries of the entail, the Squire was able to assume control of everything else left by his father.

Not long after the Squire had frustrated the wishes of his pious father, he learned that Mrs Montagu Tharp, of Chippenham Park, Newmarket, was trying to find a buyer for the Limekilns. The Limekilns, which lie in the fork of the Thetford and Bury St Edmunds roads on the eastern side of Newmarket, are, perhaps, the most famous gallops in the world, and one of the most important amenities enjoyed by the Newmarket trainers. No matter how dry the summer, the going on the Limekilns never becomes really hard.

'They can be bought, can they?' asked the Squire reflectively, fully aware of all the opportunities for mischief inherent in the situation. 'But, I wonder,' he continued, 'what the stewards would say if they knew that I was the owner?'

While the Squire revelled with unalleviated delight in the prospect of having the power to close, or even plough up, the gallops that were all but vital to Newmarket as a training centre, the Jockey Club was viewing the possibility of those gallops becoming the property of a man who was warned off with unadulterated horror. An interesting situation might have developed had not the stewards acted with a rapidity not always characteristic of them by making an offer for a lease of the ground that was acceptable to Mrs Tharp. It was not until 1930 that the Jockey Club secured the freehold of the Limekilns.

Although denied the chance to buy the Limekilns, the Squire was having no difficulty at all in finding other ways of disposing of his fortune, nor any amount of people willing to assist him in the enterprise. Henceforth he was to be the freest and fastest spender of the age, lavishing huge sums, as one Scottish newspaper so sourly put it, on 'horse racing, prize-fighting and harlotry'.

3 THE SQUIRE'S RETURN
TO THE RACECOURSE

HAVING had two years in which to cool his heels in exile from the
Turf, George Baird was both chastened and aggrieved. On the one
hand he was deeply resentful that men who had other scores to settle with
him should have been able to use their power to find him guilty of trying
to put another man over the rails – an offence of which he had been quite
innocent, notwithstanding the degree of his disrespect to the exalted party
concerned. On the other hand, he admitted to himself that he had been
guilty of rough, dirty, even dangerous riding on other occasions, and was
thoroughly ashamed of it. Although never given much to reflection, he
realized that he had often behaved in an unsportsmanlike manner. Of that
he was genuinely ashamed. He now appreciated that, contrary to what
those whom he thought his friends had told him, there was nothing in the
least smart or clever in foul riding. For what was perhaps the only time in
his life, he realized that he had allowed himself to be led astray by his
cronies.

To try to earn the reputation for being a sportsman, a reputation that
he coveted more than ever after his recent disgrace, George Baird resolved
to model himself on the last man who had been universally known as the
Squire.

This was George Osbaldeston, who had owned the Ebberston and
Allerston estates in Yorkshire. Born in 1787, Squire Osbaldeston was the
greatest all-round athlete of the first half of the last century. Pre-
eminently a horseman, who rode as well on the racecourse as he did in the

hunting field, he was also one of the best fast bowlers in the country and good enough a tennis player to be able to beat the French champion Barre. In addition, he was a first-class shot and excelled as a pugilist, besides playing an extraordinarily good game of billiards.

After being Master of the Quorn from 1817 to 1821, and again from 1823 until 1827, Squire Osbaldeston more or less forsook hunting for racing and had a large stable of horses trained by Henry Stebbings, first on his own Ebberston property, a few miles from Scarborough, and then at Hambleton near Thirsk. Osbaldeston won a lot of money by betting on himself as a match-rider, but the most famous of his bets was on a match against time. For a wager of 1,000 guineas with a Colonel Charretie, he undertook to ride two hundred miles in less than ten hours on the Saturday of the Newmarket Houghton meeting in 1831, and then struck another bet that he would do it in less than nine hours. Changing horses after every four-mile circuit of the Round Course, the Squire completed the two hundred miles in eight hours thirty-nine minutes – and then back to a large dinner at the Rutland Arms.

In due course the luck turned against the irascible little Yorkshireman. He suffered a last reverse when Rifleman was beaten by Saucebox in the St Leger of 1855, and died at the age of seventy-eight in 1865, some four years after the birth of George Baird. Although Squire Osbaldeston spent his last ten years in almost penniless obscurity, his great exploits across the fast Leicestershire country, at Newmarket and elsewhere soon became legendary and were a topic of conversation long after his death. To a young man, like George Baird, of sporting inclinations and with nothing to do but enjoy himself, Osbaldeston had to be a hero.

To identify himself with his new-found examplar, George Baird decided to adopt Squire Osbaldeston's racing colours. For some time various ladies had been telling him that his own colours, cardinal and light blue cap, clashed too much to be tasteful, but they all agreed that he would look better in the less vivid bottle-green jacket and red cap that had been worn by Osbaldeston. As it happened, though, a foreign nobleman, the Comte de Bertreux, had registered green and red cap, almost certainly without knowing their significance, with Weatherby's in 1875. George Baird therefore had to accept a slight modification by settling for green and plum cap.

As a first step towards rehabilitating himself in racing circles, George Baird set about assembling a string of high-class horses in the way that his elder cousin Douglas Baird was already doing. To this end he put his interests into the hands of thirty-eight-year-old Tom Cannon, who had been Champion Jockey in 1872 and was still at the height of his powers as a rider, although also engaged in training a big stable of horses at Danebury, near Stockbridge in Hampshire.

Tom Cannon was an exceptionally graceful horseman, with wonderful hands, so that fillies went better for him than for almost any other jockey of his day. Twice he won the Two Thousand Guineas on fillies – on Pilgrimage in 1878 and Shotover in 1882 – and his only Derby was won on Shotover. While he may not have had quite the strength of Archer in a finish, he was in no way inferior to the other as a tactician, and brought the riding of a waiting race to a fine art. A man of absolute integrity, he was born at Eton, where his father was a horse dealer, on 23rd April 1846. He was apprenticed to John Day the younger at Danebury, married Day's daughter Margaret and took over the Danebury stable at about the time of the death of his father-in-law in 1883.

At exactly the same time as George Baird was re-entering the Turf's orbit, a man who was a complete contrast to him in almost all things except the possession of a great fortune was quitting it. Evelyn Boscawen, 6th Viscount Falmouth, was looked up to by everybody as an owner in the very best tradition. He never bet, had no interest in handicaps, and was only concerned with trying to breed horses good enough to win classics at his Mereworth Castle stud near Maidstone. Having unexpectedly inherited the title from a cousin, he began racing as an owner in John Scott's Malton stable in 1857. Subsequently, he sent his horses to Mat Dawson at Heath House, Newmarket. During the thirteen years that Mat Dawson trained for him, Lord Falmouth won the Derby with Kingcraft in 1870 and Silvio in 1877, the Oaks three times and nine other classics. Almost all his important winners were ridden by Fred Archer, who had been apprenticed to Dawson before becoming his stable jockey.

Lord Falmouth's final classic success was obtained with Galliard, in the Two Thousand Guineas of 1883. On the strength of that performance, Galliard started 7/2 favourite for the Derby, only to finish third to St Blaise and Highland Chief, beaten a neck and half a length.

Racecourse rumour, never the most charitable of the media, had it that Archer had stopped Galliard to give a clear run to Highland Chief, trained and heavily backed by his brother Charlie. Lord Falmouth, according to the rumourmongers, was so disgusted by Archer's betrayal of him that he decided to give up racing and sell his horses.

The odds against there being a grain of truth in that story are very long.

It was totally out of keeping with the nature of Archer, who had too fanatical a determination to win every race, to stop a horse in a selling plate, let alone the Derby, to oblige his brother or anybody else.

Lord Falmouth's retirement from racing was nothing to do with any unwarrantable suspicion of the jockey who had served him so well. The reason was the far more prosaic one that he was growing old and the deterioration of his health was making his attendance at meetings increasingly rare.

The dispersal sale of Lord Falmouth's horses, conducted by Mr Edmund Tattersall in the paddock of Heath House on 28th April 1884, coincided with the lifting of the disqualification of the Squire almost to the day, and gave him a providential opportunity to acquire some of the best bloodstock in the world. The twenty-four broodmares included the Oaks winners, Janette, Spinaway and Wheel of Fortune, the St Leger winner, Dutch Oven, and the One Thousand Guineas winner, Cecilia, while the Derby winner, Kingcraft, was among the five stallions. In addition, there were twenty-four horses in training, sixteen yearlings and nine foals from the very best families in the *Stud Book*.

The wealth and importance of the would-be buyers did justice to the horses that Mr Tattersall had to offer them. A broad cross-section of high society crowded the Heath House paddock that April morning. The Dukes of Portland, St Albans and Hamilton were there. So were the Earls of Rosebery, Ellesmere and Zetland, Prince Soltykoff, Lord Lurgan and the Prince of Wales's racing manager, Lord Marcus Beresford.

There, too, was the tall, slim, rather awkward young man with a slight stoop, to whom nobody save his adviser Tom Cannon and his cousin Douglas Baird addressed a word. Contrary to what might seem suggested by the lack of attention paid to him, he had come shopping with more money to spend than any of the famous owners that milled around him. By the end of the day his was much the longest bill.

Not only did the Squire pay 8,800 guineas, the highest price of the sale, for the three-year-old filly Busybody, who had won the Middle Park Plate the previous autumn, but he gave 2,200 guineas for Esther Faa, a two-year-old out of Wheel of Fortune, 3,000 guineas for the yearling colt, Cerealis, 1,400 guineas for Skyscraper, another yearling colt, and 1,350 guineas for the six-year-old broodmare, Bal Gal. In all he laid out £17,587 for the foundations of the great stud that he planned to establish to help to wipe out the memory of the incidents that had brought him into disrepute.

Busybody, who was to be the first horse to carry the Squire's new colours successfully, was a superbly bred bay filly with the rare distinction of having classic winners for five of her six immediate forebears. She was by Petrarch, winner of the Two Thousand Guineas and St Leger in 1876, out of Spinaway, winner of the One Thousand Guineas and Oaks in 1876, by the 1863 Derby winner, Macaroni, out of the 1863 Oaks winner, Queen Bertha. Busybody's sire, Petrarch, was by Lord Clifden, who beat Queen Bertha in the St Leger.

Breeding pundits who believed that good gold needs an alloy may have thought her prospects badly prejudiced by such an abundance of classic winners close up in her pedigree, or they may have regarded her paternal grandam Laura, once sold for £25, as the necessary alloy. Whichever may have been the case, Busybody was able to prove that she was not too finely bred to carry on the traditions of her immediate family.

As well as the Middle Park Plate, she won two of her other three races as a two-year-old, her defeat having come when she was beaten by a neck by Queen Adelaide in the Dewhurst Stakes. Thereafter she did not race again until being bought by the Squire.

Lord Falmouth's sale having been held on the Monday of the Guineas Week, Tom Cannon had no need to remove Busybody from Newmarket immediately as she was to fulfil her engagement in the One Thousand Guineas the following Friday. Starting favourite for that race at 85/40, with Tom Cannon replacing Fred Archer in the saddle, she took her revenge on Queen Adelaide, whom she beat half a length. On taking her back to Danebury, Cannon kept her there until sending her to Epsom for the Oaks, in which she justified odds of 21/20 on by beating Superba half a length with her old rival Queen Adelaide a bad third.

At that stage of his career, the Squire had not acquired the disdain for the fashionable meetings which he was so soon to show, and, having won both the One Thousand Guineas and the Oaks, he was impatient for Busybody to bring him fresh glory by winning at Royal Ascot. Tom Cannon was far from enthusiastic about taking the pitcher to the well again so soon. The gallops at Danebury were becoming increasingly firm as spring turned into summer, and it was only too plain to him that Busybody hated the ground. The Squire, though, insisted on her being prepared for the Royal Meeting, and inevitably she broke down. She never ran again, but having won a classic on each of her two appearances under the Squire's new colours, she had already proved herself cheap at the price he paid for her.

The other part of the Squire's plan to redeem his reputation on the Turf involved his becoming as competent a rider under Jockey Club rules as he had been in hunters' flat races and over hurdles. With this end in view, he learned all he could from Tom Cannon when riding work at Danebury. It was from Cannon he learned how to ride a waiting race. At times he was inclined to delay his challenge too long, and that was to be regarded as his principal shortcoming as a race-rider.

In the season of his reinstatement, the Squire's string was more notable for its quality, as principally exemplified by Busybody, than the quantity that would be so much its salient characteristic in another two years' time. As a consequence of his having relatively few horses from which to provide himself with mounts, he was unable to ride regularly in 1884, and although he was back in the saddle almost as soon as he ceased to be a disqualified person, success was not immediately forthcoming. For a number of weeks the best that he could do was to reach a place. Three days after Busybody had won the Oaks, he was second on Student, beaten half a length by Archer's mount, on a return to Four Oaks Park, the scene of his personal disaster of two years previously, but it was not until the August Bank Holiday that he broke his duck. In those days, the Metropolitan Bank Holiday meeting used to be held on what they called the Great Welcomes course at Croydon, where racing was discontinued after 1890. It was there that he obtained his first riding success under Jockey Club rules on Carrodus, running in the name of the Chilton, Berkshire, trainer, William Stevens. Carrodus, who was the even money favourite, beat Rocket by eight lengths with Dormouse last of three in a two-mile selling plate. Even when, at last, he was first past the post, the Squire had to survive an objection for going the wrong course, by Dan Thirlwell, a fellow amateur. The Squire also won on Carrodus at Warwick about three weeks later, and at the Croydon autumn meeting in October.

Although unable to take very many more mounts in the second half of 1884 than he had in the first, the Squire enjoyed considerably greater success. In the middle of October he brought off a double on Cylinder, running in the name of his friend 'Stiffy' Smith, and Lord Rossmore's Helicon at Worcester; then early in November, had another double on his own horse, Round Shot, and on Robert Peck's Poste Restante at Shrewsbury, thereby bringing his score for the season to thirteen.

Leaving aside considerations of superstition, thirteen winners in a season curtailed by his being a disqualified person during the early part of it was an extremely satisfactory bag. Furthermore, he was also the owner of the winners of nine races, of which two were classics. Very far from being content with these results, the Squire was considerably disgruntled and bitterly disappointed. The olive branch he had held out to the Establishment had been pointedly ignored. As became a man of his means, he had laid out his money to buy the best horses on the market, had them trained by a man of impeccable character and been scrupulously careful to give no offence by his own riding. Yet members of the Jockey Club, their families and friends still treated him with cold indifference at best, and all too often with open hostility.

Not for him the friendship shown to his cousin Douglas, who was becoming increasingly important in racing circles. Even after he had won the Oaks, there was hardly a murmur of congratulation. He felt as though the hands of all men were turned against him, or, at least, the hands of all those who had even the lightest grip on the reins of power. The Jockey Club, he felt, had taken up an attitude of relentless antipathy towards him, despite his having had his punishment and shown his willingness to race on the same lines as its members did, and, in the case of at least one of them, on very much straighter lines.

The trouble was that, at the age of twenty-two, and that is all he was, he could not understand that bridges have to be rebuilt from both sides of a chasm. It is a process which takes a long time – so much time, in fact, that a man who sows a bushel of wild oats in unguided youth can be middle-aged before he is accepted by an Establishment that feels itself betrayed by him. To Baird's mind, a unilateral declaration of respectability on his part was more than enough to mend the bridge. He simply could not understand why it had not been his passport to the position in the social order to which his millions entitled him. Nor did it seem to occur to him that his addiction to roistering around the West End, Newmarket and the surrounding villages, or anywhere else where he might happen to be, was hardly a recommendation for entry into more sophisticated society. People were waiting for him to grow up, which was something he never did. All his life he was the boy who had roamed the countryside around Stichil, untutored and resentful of even the mildest restraint, but generous and anxious to please. The pity was that he generally tried to please the wrong people.

To some extent, the course of George Baird's life was dictated as much by his exclusion from the social circle of his fellow plutocrats as by his natural inclinations. As a result of what he resentfully saw as undeserved rejection, he would be a hell-raiser and a whoremaster, riding hard, betting high, drinking heavily and treating women with much less consideration than he did his horses. The image of Squire Osbaldeston was fast fading from his mind as he began to invite comparison with another squire, Jack Mytton, the harum-scarum squire of Halston, Shropshire, who had died penniless at the age of thirty-seven back in 1834.

Still hardly of age, George Baird had already enjoyed two of the greatest triumphs the British Turf can offer only to be left with a sour taste in his mouth as a result of the indifference with which they were received. He did not care if he never owned another important winner, especially as success could be obtained by the simple process of writing a cheque. Riding winners, though, was a very different matter. Now that he had acquired some of the technique and a measure of the subtlety of Cannon, winning races gave him an exhilaration that nothing else could do. He may not have managed to cultivate any of the social graces, but he was not the raw youth who had cut his teeth in hunters' flat races in the North and Midlands. Instead he was becoming an exceedingly competent Gentleman Rider, who was a match for all but the best of professionals.

In those days, Gentlemen Riders had far more scope on the flat than the amateurs of the present day. Having obtained permission from the stewards of the Jockey Club to ride on even terms with professionals and paid £5 to the Bentinck Benevolent Fund, they could take a mount in any race they pleased, except one for apprentices. What prevented almost all of them from riding in the Derby or other big races was their inability to do the weight, not restrictions imposed by the rules of racing. Mr George Thursby was one of the few who could get down to less than the 9 stones horses carry in the Derby, and he not only rode in it but was second on both John O'Gaunt in 1904 and Picton in 1906.

Although not as light as George Thursby, the Squire was able to make extensive use of the permission to ride against professionals. Towards the end of the nineteenth century, horses were racing under both very low weights, like, for instance, the 5 stone 11 pounds at which H. Arnull won on Mechlin at Yarmouth in July 1885, and very high weights. At all but the most important meetings, there were a lot of welter handicaps in which the top weight was generally in excess of 10 stone, and welter plates in which the same sort of burden was carried, while the conditions of weight-for-age races usually required four-year-olds and upwards to carry between 9 stone 11 pounds and 10 stone 4 pounds.

Furthermore, weights in selling races tended to be high, and there were many more such events than there are at the present time. Two sellers on one card was normal, three far from uncommon, and on some occasions there were even four.

As well as being able to ride against professional jockeys, the Gentlemen Riders had their own races. Meetings like those at Brighton and Lewes on the Sussex circuit and Stockbridge, where the Bibury Club held its annual fixture, went out of their way to provide opportunities for Gentlemen Riders, either by staging races confined to them or framing races with conditions requiring horses ridden by jockeys to carry penalties.

When sober, which was not always the case, the Squire could be in unbeatable form in the Gentlemen Riders' races, and the public followed his mounts blindly. Winning races against his peers, and the ease with which he could demonstrate the superiority of his skill, always afforded him much satisfaction, but by far his greatest pleasure lay in wiping the eye of one of the senior jockeys. After the days of Busybody and his abortive attempt to enter the ranks of the leading owners, it could truly be said of him that he would rather have beaten Archer by a short head in a seller at Worcester than have owned the winner of the Triple Crown ridden by a professional.

Having given his heart to riding winners, he devoted his fortune to the same end. Just as other rich men collected pictures, furniture or exotic plants, the Squire was an avid collector of racehorses. Whenever he saw a selling race, he bought the winner. When a horse was for sale privately, he could usually be relied upon to pay the asking price, no matter how extortionate it might be. Through his continual expenditure on bloodstock, the Squire completely dominated what he had made a sellers' market, much to the chagrin of other Gentlemen Riders of more moderate means such as Major Harding Cox, who complained they had no chance of buying a decent horse at a reasonable price.

Nobody knew how many horses the Squire owned. Certainly he had no idea himself.

'Yes, there are a lot of them at one place or another,' he once remarked in a nonchalant masterpiece of understatement, 'but exactly how many there are, I'm damned if I know.'

Just occasionally he would go into reverse by giving one or two away. A whisky distiller called Jenkins wanted to cut a dash at the Midlothian Yeomanry's meeting at Musselburgh and asked the Squire to sell him a couple of horses. The Squire, with that impetuous generosity which was typical of him, would not accept any money. Instead he said to Jenkins, 'Take this note to W. G. Stevens at Compton and pick any two horses out of the lot he trains for me.'

Buying, though, was usually the Squire's game. He regarded his money as inexhaustible and never so well spent as on something that would give him a winning ride. Whether it was at Kempton Park, Windsor or one of the other London meetings, or on a course in the remote countryside, was of absolutely no consequence at all. On one memorable occasion he went to the expense of hiring a whole train to take him to one of the lesser northern meetings for a fancied ride in a seller.

The important meetings like Royal Ascot, Newmarket, York and Goodwood he virtually ignored. Those were the courses frequented by members of society, whether or not they knew anything about racing. Still worse, the weights were far too low to allow participation by Gentlemen Riders. Such interest as he did take in those fashionable meetings was aroused by the opportunity for punting. A tilt at the ring never came amiss to him, but backing winners was in his book always a very poor second to riding them.

4 THE SQUIRE AND
FRED ARCHER

ONLY the best being good enough for the Squire, it was inevitable that he would turn to Fred Archer for tuition in jockeyship. This he did in the autumn of 1884, despite all that Tom Cannon achieved for him since his reinstatement on the Turf. Not only had Archer been undisputed champion for ten years, but his dashing, flashing style, his whip flourishing in a driving finish, was far better calculated to catch the imagination of an impressionable young man than the purposeful restraint of Cannon.

Since Archer out of the saddle had none of the flamboyance characteristic of him in it, he and the Squire might have seemed far too incompatible in temperament and outlook to have anything but the most perfunctory of relationships. Archer was introspective, abstemious and business-like. The Squire, on the other hand, was brash, self-indulgent and absurdly casual, but he did have two things for which the champion jockey had a profound respect. One was money. They did not call Fred 'The Tinman' for nothing ('tin' being the current slang for money). The other was determination to win all the races he could, no matter how far he had to travel or how great the expense involved. Whereas the genius of Archer enabled him to get almost any mount he wanted, the Squire relied upon his money, either buying fancied horses outright or paying another rider to stand down while putting the owner on to the odds to £200 or more. Money meant absolutely nothing to him when there was a winner to be ridden. Like Archer, the Squire, at that time, seemed to regard the riding of as many winners as possible as the performance of a sacred duty that could never be completely fulfilled but never abandoned.

Archer rode his first winner for the Squire on the two-year-old filly Jenny at Lichfield on 16th September 1884. Shortly afterwards the Squire suggested that they should go into partnership. He would buy or rent a Newmarket stable, which they would run together, with Archer riding the horses in their most important engagements while he rode them in the others when the weights permitted.

At that time, first claim on Archer was held by the Duke of Portland and Lord Hastings, the principal patrons of the Heath House, Newmarket, stable of Mat Dawson, to whom the champion had been apprenticed. The Duke of Portland had never been best pleased by Archer riding for the Squire, and when he came to hear rumours about their joining forces he behaved as though he had received a personal insult.

Although no more than twenty-seven years of age, Portland already regarded himself as the guardian of the interests of the Establishment. The mere idea of a man recently warned off having a prior claim on the champion jockey to his ducal self and lordly confederate could have been enough to give him an apoplectic fit. Spared such a visitation, he summoned Archer to inform him that he would not stand for his jockey having any sort of arrangement with Abington Baird and that the association was to cease forthwith. To this Archer, a man of strong, independent character, replied that the duke had better find another jockey as he proposed to ride for whom he pleased when his retainers had been honoured. There the matter had to rest. If the Squire ever knew that he had been the cause of the Duke of Portland's losing the services of the greatest jockey in the world, he would have been immensely gratified.

Having completely severed his lucrative connection with the Duke of Portland, Archer did not accept the proposition of the Squire in its entirety, allowing the idea of their running a stable together to drop. He was, however, perfectly willing to ride for him regularly and coach him in jockeyship. In view of the high price that Archer put upon his services and the willingness with which the Squire paid up when he wanted something badly enough, this tuition must have been the most expensive set of riding lessons in history.

Hardly had Fred Archer broken with Portland than he suffered a tragedy of such magnitude that his highly strung nervous system never gave him a chance of recovering from the horror of its impact. He had just won the Liverpool Autumn Cup on the Duchess of Montrose's Thebais at

Aintree on 6th November when he received a telegram saying that his young wife Nellie had given birth to a daughter. Elated, he hurried home to Newmarket only to find Nellie convulsed by an agony in which she died without recognizing him.

Even though his daughter was saved, nothing could console Fred Archer for the death of his beloved wife. Thenceforward he was a broken man, beyond the reach of all those who sought to comfort him. A winter holiday in the United States did nothing to revive his spirits, and it was in the depths of the same despair that he had left that he returned to Newmarket just before the opening of the season of 1885, to ride work for the stables with which he was associated and to continue with the coaching of the Squire.

Riding gallops together in the biting east wind that whipped across to Newmarket from the North Sea in that early spring of 1885, the professional imparting the wiles and subleties of his trade to the multi-millionaire, the Squire and Archer would have been a readily recognizable pair. Each was a head or more taller than the diminutive figures to be seen on most of the other horses on the heath of a morning, so that, sitting well back in their saddles with legs thrust forward in their long stirrups of the old style, theirs were about the only heels protruding beneath the bodies of their horses. The physical resemblance that he bore to Archer was largely responsible for the Squire being able to mould his style on that of the champion, just as, some fifteen years earlier, Archer had been able to imitate his own mentor, poor Tom French, a hard, strong jockey who had died of tuberculosis at the age of twenty-nine in 1873.

Archer and the Squire shared their first success of 1885 when the heavily backed Round Shot won at Liverpool on the fourth day of the season. Back north for Manchester's Whitsun meeting, Archer rode the Squire's McMahon to win the £1,000 Salford Borough Handicap, which remained one of the most important sprints in the country until racing at Manchester finished, and in November he rode his fifteenth and final winner of the year for the Squire on Arbaces at Northampton.

In a three-horse race for a five-furlong seller, Arbaces beat Scotch Pearl by three parts of a length, with Lord Ellesmere's Housewife a length away third. The Squire had to go to 350 guineas, a big price for a moderate horse in those days, to retain Arbaces, while Lord Ellesmere claimed Scotch Pearl on behalf of Archer. During the last sad year of Archer's life, Scotch Pearl, a grey mare by Strathconan, was his favourite hack.

Archer had also won on Arbaces at Nottingham in the spring, and on the second day of that meeting the Squire had obtained his first riding success of 1885 on Lyric. In July, he rode his tenth winner of the season on Leoville, one of the horses still running in the name of his parasitic friend, 'Stiffy' Smith, at Worcester. The following month he paid a brief visit to the continent to ride at the German spa town of Baden-Baden, taking with him two of his horses, Plutarch and Beau Nash.

Although the Victorian equivalent of the jet set had to be content with far slower transports than its modern counterpart, they did make frequent use of channel steamers and still more luxuriously appointed railway trains to visit the fashionable continental resorts of which Baden-Baden was a particular favourite. Situated in the Black Forest in the Grand Duchy of Baden, Baden-Baden retained its popularity long after the closure of the casino, which had financed the construction of the town's splendid public buildings, in about 1875. In the late summer of every year, members of the high society of Austria, Germany, Russia, France and Britain assembled there to partake a wide variety of pleasures. Day after day, until well into the autumn, they were to be seen driving along the tree-lined Lichtenthaler Allee, taking the water at the hot springs, strolling among the bandstands, neo-classical pavilions and cafés in the public gardens, the Conversations-Haus, or racing on the course at the little village of Iffezheim, about an hour's drive from the town.

British influence almost dominated the Baden-Baden race meetings, as may be seen from the names of the professional jockeys riding at them: Busby, Jeffrey, Ballantine, Grimshaw, Watts, Smith and Clough. In addition, many of the most celebrated of the Anglo-Irish Gentleman Riders used to take mounts at the international meeting in late August. Others besides the Squire riding there in 1885 included Dan Thirlwell, brother-in-law of the Newmarket trainer Richard Marsh, John Beasley, uncle of Rufus Beasley, and one of the Moore brothers.

The Squire made a disheartening start to this continental venture, as his first mount, Plutarch, was disqualified for crossing after having passed the post first, a length ahead of the mount of a professional called Sear, in the Stadt Preis. A few days later, the Squire had ample compensation for that initial set-back when he rode Beau Nash to win the local St leger. For all the grandeur of its name, that race was only a mile and a quarter handicap, which could not have taken much winning as the Squire had bought Beau Nash out of a seller at the Newmarket Craven meeting.

Back in England the following week, the Squire won in his own colours on Kimbolton at Derby. Later in September, he made what was to become an annual pilgrimage back to his own country to ride at the Ayr Western meeting, where he won on Bob Peck's Hungarian on the second day and a Mr Craig's Engadine on the third.

The last of the twenty-two winners that 'Mr Abington' rode under Jockey Club rules in 1885 was Herald at Warwick on 23rd November. Herald ran in the name of his trainer, the former steeplechase jockey, Teddy Weever, who had a mixed stable at Bourton-on-the-Hill, Gloucestershire.

In the spring of 1886, Fred Archer was again riding regularly in the green jacket and plum cap of 'Mr Abington', for whom he had two mounts at the opening meeting at Lincoln, being second on Kimbolton on the Tuesday and unplaced on Alarm in the Brocklesby Stakes the following afternoon. Alarm was a bay colt by Peter. By trying to register the horse as Cock Crow, the Squire had succeeded in giving fresh offence to the more devout members of the Jockey Club.

The Squire's only runner at Liverpool in the second half of the opening week of the 1886 season was Kimbolton, on whom Archer was runner-up in the Spring Cup on the Saturday. Two days earlier, the Squire had bought Bob Peck's Tommy Upton out of Liverpool's optional seller for 380 guineas, thereby securing one of his relatively few bargains. As he and the former trainer, Bob Peck, were becoming increasingly friendly, it seems more than likely that he actually bought the horse on Peck's advice.

On the Thursday of the next week, the Squire won on Shrivenham, owned by the bookmaker Charlie Hibbert, on the now long-defunct course at Croxton Park, Leicestershire. The following day racing moved to Leicester's new course at Oadby Park, where Archer, putting up 1 pound overweight at 8 stone 10 pounds, won a breeders' foal stakes on the Squire's Binder.

After Binder, Archer rode just one more winner in the Squire's colours. That was En Jacme, who was allowed to go for 130 guineas after beating Matrimony by two lengths in a seller at the Chester meeting in early May.

As the Squire had an abiding aversion to losing any horse, he would not have been best pleased at En Jacme being sold out of his stable, which was probably done in his absence since Chester was one of those meetings he disdained by reason of the weights being too low to allow him to ride. Therefore there is a possibility that Archer was looking after his interests there, and that the sale of En Jacme was the cause of a quarrel between them. For the remainder of 1886, the Squire relied upon the services of

Tom Cannon's former apprentice, Jack Watts, as well as Ben Loates and Charlie Wood; and, in the North, on Jim Fagan, who won him the Cumberland Plate on Ben Alder. He also took an ever-increasing number of mounts himself after having looked in imminent danger of making a second enforced departure from the Turf in the late spring.

Riding his black mare Lovely in a five-furlong handicap at Kempton Park on 8th May, he finished third of five to the odds-on favourite Repps, on whom Archer won by twelve lengths. For reasons they did not specify, the Stewards called 'Mr Abington' before them to explain his riding, and, not being satisfied, reported him to the stewards of the Jockey Club. Having had one taste of the stewards' summary justice four years earlier, the Squire can hardly have been sanguine about the outcome of his case, especially as he had, in the meantime, succeeded in doing nothing at all to endear himself to the Establishment for all the good intentions with which he had returned to the Turf's fold.

Fortunately for the Squire, the deep misgivings he must have had proved quite unfounded. However much they may have disapproved of his personal life, the stewards of the Jockey Club, Lord Hastings, Lord Suffolk and Mr H. W. Fitzwilliam, could find no fault with his riding at Kempton Park, and 'acquitted Mr Abington of any intention of Fraud'. The very wording of the findings suggests that the Kempton stewards had made very serious allegations, but the use of the word 'Fraud' renders it inconceivable that he was guilty as charged. Whatever else he might have done the Squire would never have thrown away a race. On the contrary, as everyone, except those in the rarefied atmosphere of Kempton's stewards' box knew, he would pay huge sums of money for just one winning mount.

Apart from that disagreeable incident at Kempton, the season of 1886 was a good one for the Squire. Not only did he ride winners rather more regularly than he had during the preceding season, but his horses also won frequently in the hands of the professionals, bringing off more than the occasional gamble.

Tommy Upton showed how well he had been bought out of that Liverpool seller in the spring by winning for Charlie Wood at Epsom and Windsor, and twice in two days for Ben Loates at Newton (from whence the races were to be transferred to near-by Haydock Park in 1898).

In the autumn, Tommy Upton was taken back to Epsom, where he gave the Squire his first riding success there by winning a six-furlong sprint for Gentleman Riders by three lengths. Knowing that the gradients of Epsom provided the supreme test of jockeyship, and that it was the course on which Archer excelled above all others, winning that race on Tommy Upton gave the Squire infinitely more pleasure than the sight of Tom Cannon riding Busybody to win the Oaks had done. If he were in the saddle, sellers always counted for more than classics with the Squire.

Archer himself handled Epsom with all his accustomed skill at that meeting, notwithstanding the desperate trouble he was having with his weight. So serious had his problem become that he had to put up overweight on both his mounts, riding Captain Machell's Devea at 8 stone 12 pounds on the first day and getting down to a pound less for the Duchess of Montrose's Gay Hermit on the second. Nevertheless, he won a close-run race on Devea, forcing her home by a head from the mount of Charlie Wood.

While his misery was multiplied by the physical hardship involved in trying to control his weight that autumn, the only thing to which Archer could look forward with the slightest degree of pleasure was winning the Cambridgeshire on the Duchess of Montrose's St Mirin. The Cambridge-shire was the only important race he had never won, and the duchess and her friends were already backing St Mirin as though they were using other people's money. The trouble was that St Mirin was set to carry 8 stone 6 pounds, and every extra pound on his back would jeopardize his chance in the most open handicap of the season.

Archer was absolutely certain that he would not be beaten by inability to do the weight or anything else. A few days before the race, he said to Harry Custance, the former jockey, ''Cus I am sure to ride St Mirin at 8 stone 6 pounds, or 8 stone 7 pounds, and I shall win the Cambridgeshire,' while, with surer prophecy, he told another friend, 'I have never ridden the winner of the Cambridgeshire, and if I don't succeed this time, I shall never try again.'

Following days of agony, Archer weighed out at 8 stone 7 pounds for the Cambridgeshire, but the extra pound cost him the race. After he had taken St Mirin into the lead inside the distance, the Sailor Prince, ridden by 'Tiny' White, came through with a late challenge on the far rails to win by a head.

The biggest winner over the race was the Squire. Whereas the other patrons of W. G. Stevens's stable had followed their trainer's advice by having a modest interest, the Squire, as was his custom when one of his trainers had a fancied runner, had put a few hundred pounds on. The only other notable punter to win well over The Sailor Prince, who started at

22/1, was the Prince of Wales. He backed the horse because of its name, his brother Alfred, Duke of Edinburgh, being a naval officer.

As was inevitable, the defeat of St Mirin intensified the despair and world-weariness felt by Archer. Worse still, the privations that he had been undergoing to keep his weight in check began to take their toll now that he was having to expose his emaciated body to the cold autumn winds. Despite his having caught a chill at that fateful Cambridgeshire meeting, he insisted on riding again the following week, until he was taken seriously ill and almost collapsed at Lewes on the Thursday. The following Monday, 8th November 1886, he shot himself in a fit of delirium.

Whatever lessons the Squire may have learned from the example of Fred Archer, the dangers of excessive wasting was not one of them. Although the man he admired most in the world had just been driven to suicide as a result of having tried to live on a diet so drastic as to be one step from starvation, the Squire showed himself no mercy in his own equally inflexible determination to do light. At the meeting at Derby in the middle of November, men who could not afford a good winter coat saw the richest commoner in the kingdom shivering in a thin silk shirt rather than put up more than the minimum overweight on Ironclad, and all to no avail. Riding at 9 stone 9 pounds, which was three pounds overweight, he finished unplaced.

Five days later he was able to ride Malvern at the much more comfortable weight of 10 stone 3 pounds and win by the equally comfortable margin of ten lengths at Warwick.

On the second day of that Warwick meeting, the Squire rode his twenty-eighth and final winner of 1886 on Jack Hammond's Strathblane.

The pattern for the next few years of the Squire's life was set. Nothing was to stop him winning races. No matter how little he could eat nor how much he had to pay, he must ride winners. To the sporting ambitions inspired in him by his first hero, Squire Osbaldeston, had been added the fanaticism of Fred Archer.

The Squire thought of Archer as the man who had taught him how to live. The dreadful irony was that the champion had shown him the way to die. Had the Squire not wasted every bit as hard as Archer had used to do, his constitution would never have been so badly undermined that he was left with no resistance to his final illness.

5 NEWMARKET

ANY house-party given by the Squire at Bedford Lodge, Newmarket, bore more resemblance to a localized riot than any known form of social gathering. More than one man with a broad mind and a strong stomach curtailed a week-end there of his own volition long before Monday morning had come.

Soon after Busybody had completed the double in the fillies' classics of 1884, the Squire decided that he must have his own trainer in his own stable. There was, of course, no question of Tom Cannon becoming his private trainer. Even if his career in the saddle had finished, it is inconceivable that his character and sound commercial instincts would have allowed him to act in that capacity for any owner, let alone one as fickle and capricious as the Squire.

The Squire therefore leased the Bedford Lodge establishment from Captain Machell and installed Martin Gurry as his trainer while continuing to keep horses in other yards all over the country. Bedford Lodge, which is now one of the best hotels in East Anglia, lies a little way up the Bury Road on the eastern side of Newmarket. A large, more or less rectangular country house with white elevations, it has tall elegant windows but a somewhat low-pitched slate roof that seems to disguise its height.

As their names infer, Bedford Lodge and the next-door Bedford Cottage stable were once the property of the Dukes of Bedford. Their original Newmarket house had been hardly more than a small rural retreat set further back from the Bury Road. This was replaced by the more imposing Bedford Lodge at some time around the end of the eighteenth century. The 5th Duke, who won the Derby three times between 1789 and 1797, was a great racing man, but neither his brother and successor nor the latter's son, the 7th Duke, had much taste for the Turf. On the death of the 7th Duke in 1861, Bedford Lodge was sold to the Scottish trainer, Joseph Dawson, who built the stableyard, with its large, airy cage boxes, to the east of the house in 1864. Dawson died in 1880, and soon afterwards house and stable were acquired by his neighbour, Captain Machell, who had the Bedford Cottage stable.

James Octavius Machell, the Squire's Newmarket landlord, came of an old Westmorland family though he had been born at Beverley in the East Riding of Yorkshire, the son of a clergyman, in 1838. As a young man he had been a splendid athlete, capable of jumping over a billiard table or on to a mantelpiece from a standstill. Disappointed at having been too young to go to the Crimean War and at a lack of subsequent opportunities for active service, he resigned his commission in the army to devote himself to racing. Soon he was managing a big stable of horses at Bedford Cottage, where, first, the brothers Charles and George Bloss, and later Joe Cannon, Jimmy Jewett and others trained for him. Outwardly, at any rate, a hard, calculating and extremely suspicious man, he made a great deal of money out of betting and the buying and selling of horses, so that he was able to buy back the family home in Westmorland in addition to purchasing much other property.

At the time when the Squire was there, Newmarket was a much smaller and more compact town than it is today. To the east there were very few buildings beyond Bedford Lodge and Sefton Lodge, which more or less stands opposite it on the Bury Road. Living at Sefton Lodge was that formidable lady, Caroline, Duchess of Montrose.

A large woman, much given to wearing clothes of a masculine cut, the duchess was known behind her ample back as Six Mile Bottom, a village a few miles from Newmarket, or Carrie Red, on account of the colour of her hair. Caroline Agnes, daughter of 2nd Lord Decies, had married the 4th Duke of Montrose in 1836. Soon after his death in 1874, she took as her second husband Mr W. S. Stirling-Crawfurd, who won the 1878 Derby with Sefton and a lot of other races with horses trained by old Alec Taylor at Manton.

The duchess, who retained her title after marrying again, shared Stirling-Crawfurd's enthusiasm for racing, but as even she would not break the convention that women did not have horses in their own names, she ran them in the thinly disguised one of 'Mr Manton'. Strong-willed and imperious in manner, with an acid tongue, she was the terror of her frequently changed trainers and jockeys. Few had the courage of the lightweight Harry Huxtable, who, on being asked why he had not come when she had told him to, blandly replied, 'I beg your pardon, Your Grace, but I should have had to come without the horse.'

Two such forceful characters as Captain Machell and the duchess were bound to clash from time to time, and, as often or not, they were on the worst possible terms. When the captain ran over her favourite dog in his fly, she elaborated upon the incident by declaring that he had raised himself from the seat to come down as hard as he could above the axle to be sure of killing the poor animal.

While captain and duchess carried on their feuds amid intermittent periods of truce and friendship, their young neighbour made himself more talked about than either of them down in the town by his extraordinary behaviour at Bedford Lodge. Reigning like a king in a motley court, the Squire, at the still tender age of twenty-four, found absolutely no shortage of encouragement in the worst excesses of his folly.

Whenever the Squire sent word that he was coming into residence at Bedford Lodge, those of his minions who had been eating the bread of idleness, or, more literally, drinking the wine of the same, bestirred themselves to make ready for his arrival. Those preparations were not of quite the same order as those that preceded the return of any other Victorian millionaire to his country seat. For days on end the roughs and toughs, euphemistically known as secretaries, of his Newmarket staff scoured the lanes and by-ways of the town and surrounding villages like Cheveley, Fordham, Saxon Street and Soham, looking for stray dogs, the wilder and more savage the better, to be matched in mortal combat with the Squire's favourite Staffordshire bull terrier, an abominable beast by the name of Donald. Few things were better calculated to amuse the young master, with his primitive passion for noise, violence and the occasional bloodbath, than a good dog-fight of an evening.

The same partialities accounted for the Squire's addiction to cock-fighting. Thus, while the dog-catchers went about their nefarious business, the keepers of his fighting cocks put their birds on to intensive diets to prime them for the main. Cock-fighting had been made illegal in Great Britain as early as 1849, though it has continued clandestinely in certain areas down to the present day.

Of the many hostelries that flourished in Newmarket during the late Victorian era, the one most favoured by the Squire was the Greyhound, which, until it was pulled down in about 1895, stood on the site now occupied by the defunct Doric Cinema in the High Street. An old coaching inn, which had been made redundant for its original purpose by the coming of the railway line, the Greyhound had a long, narrow bar with a raftered ceiling, sawdust spread upon the floor and deal tables set along its length. It was around those tables that every conceivable kind of roguery and villainy had been plotted, even long before the name of racing had seemed irretrievably tarnished.

Since the inn continued to cater for its share of doubtful characters, the Squire and his companions would have been much amused by its clientele. The other attraction of the place, besides the companionship engendered by the heavy drinking and earthy humour of the smoke-filled bar, was the fighting room that the landlord, Bill Riley, kept at the back of the premises. It was there that Jem Smith sparred with Charlie Mitchell while training for his fight with Jake Kilrain in 1887.

All sorts of fighting men frequented the Greyhound, some, like Jem Mace and Tom King, being in their prime, some, like Tom Sayers, the smallest of all English champions, being old and penniless, while others were also down on their luck but still capable of fighting. To these Bill Riley would give a much-needed meal, saying, 'Here, sleep on that sofa, you fight tomorrow.' Word would go round Newmarket that there was to be a fight behind the Greyhound, and in the evening a large crowd of stable lads, jockeys and a small group of trainers, often including Mat Dawson, an enthusiastic connoisseur of the ring, would assemble around Bill Riley's arena to see the sport.

Alternatively, that back room of the Greyhound was used for cock-fighting, or dog-fights between vicious, red bull terriers that were kept for that purpose. All these sports being dear to the heart of the Squire, he soon became a regular patron of the inn and a close friend of Charlie Mitchell, Jem Smith and the rest of the prize-fighters who haunted it.

Although Bill Riley could cater for his tastes so admirably in the back room of the Greyhound, the Squire decided that he should have his own private boxing saloon. Accordingly, a large room was built on to the western side of Bedford Lodge. On the outer wall of this extension were placed two medallions, depicting scenes from the classics in relief, embellishments that reflected the culture of the architect rather than of the young man on whose mind the masters of Eton and the dons of Cambridge had been able to make no impact at all.

Having acquired his own boxing saloon, the Squire set about enlarging his private circus of prize-fighters who would live at his expense and train on the facilities that he provided. The manifold duties of these gentlemen included the instruction of their patron into the Noble Art and acting as his bodyguards when it was his pleasure to indulge in a piece of particularly intensive hell-raising. Among the first fighters to join the Squire's circus were Charlie Mitchell and Jem Smith, neither of whom could be expected to introduce any elements of gracious living into Bedford Lodge, where they competed for a share of the action with a gang of shameless London layabouts and some decidedly colourful ladies, who were a good deal better acquainted with ease than virtue.

To this unprepossessing assortment, almost all of whom were as much bereft of talent as integrity, it was the Squire's pleasure to play host. Bedford Lodge was Liberty Hall with a vengeance. He was as free with the champagne that he loved as with the lesser wines, the brandy and cigars and all that was needed for the table, to say nothing of the 'loans' that were forthcoming on the flimsiest of pretexts, or very often no pretext at all.

Puffing away at expensive cigars, with drinks slopping out of glasses held at all sorts of perilous angles, inebriated heavyweights sprawled gracelessly on sofas and settees, which, though of sturdy Victorian design, were often in imminent danger of collapse. Conversation took the form of ridiculing the Establishment in general and the Jockey Club in particular, and the retailing and embroidering of the most salacious of the current gossip for the delectation of the Squire.

Few of the guests could ever refrain from airing their colossal ignorance of racing, and night after night they proffered their advice on how his horses should be ridden and trained, or else they laid fatuous plans for spectacular betting coups. Alternatively, the desultory and drunken chatter would veer round to boxing as some worn-out pug revived the distant past by rambling on about one of the few fights that he had won, while others, without even the tattered remnants of glory, compensated themselves with the invention of careers in the ring. Eventually one sportsman would challenge the truth of a claim made by another sportsman and yet another brawl would be under way.

Bottles, glasses, expensive furniture and, quite often, bones would all get broken. The Squire, far from being annoyed by the debris created by

TOP: *Busybody, the first good horse owned by the Squire, at stud. She won him the 1,000 Guineas and The Oaks and bred Meddler*

CENTRE: *the well-named Meddler, a son of Busybody, who might have won a second Derby for the Squire* THE BRITISH RACEHORSE

LEFT: *Gallinule, the sire of Pretty Polly, was the most important horse ever owned or ridden by the Squire, who sold him at a substantial loss* THE BRITISH RACEHORSE

Spinjing 'em on "The Hill".

The Bar
in trou

Light refreshment for the Winner

*Merry Hampton and impressions of Epsom on the day he won the Derby of 1887 for
the Squire, as seen by the artist of the 'Illustrated Sporting and Dramatic News'*
ILLUSTRATED LONDON NEWS

After crossing the road.

merry Hampton took the lead.

Eiridsford. dropped back.

Coming home — Block on Balham Hill.

ABOVE LEFT: *October 1886, the final appearance of Fred Archer in the paddock at Newmarket. He was pleased to give the Squire what must have been the most expensive riding lessons in history* MARY EVANS PICTURE LIBRARY

ABOVE RIGHT: *the Squire's first mentor on the Turf, Tom Cannon, who trained and rode Busybody to win him the 1,000 Guineas and the Oaks in 1884*

BELOW LEFT: *Sammy Loates, whose riding could be almost as foul as his language, one of the Squire's favourite jockeys*

BELOW CENTRE: *poker-faced Jack Watts rode Merry Hampton to win the Derby for the Squire in 1887*

BELOW RIGHT: *Fred Webb, welter-weight jockey and notably strong finisher, against whom the Squire rode a dead heat on Mirabeau at Liverpool in July 1890*

the fracas, was hugely amused by the handiwork of his ruffians and played the part of Lord of Misrule with undisguised relish. Life, as Lord Lonsdale would have said, was lovely fun.

Although an alcoholic chaos dominated the domestic scene at Bedford Lodge, there was nevertheless a semblance of routine by reason of the Squire being genuinely dedicated to race riding. While the lads in the yard were making ready the first lot of horses in the early morning, the Squire would be wakened by his valet, George Monk, no matter how late he had gone to bed, to take a cup of weak tea and cod-liver oil, which was all the breakfast that he allowed himself for fear of putting on weight – a prospect that he viewed with as much horror as any professional jockey.

Having partaken of that light refreshment, the Squire would ride out of the yard in the grey light of dawn, reins held loosely in the right hand and mounted on the quietest of hacks. Like Fred Archer, who had his beloved old grey plater Scotch Pearl, and many other famous horsemen, the Squire loathed riding anything that was not quiet enough to be a child's first pony unless he was on the racecourse or the gallops.

One of his hacks cost him £700. When the animal became fractious and irritable the first time that he rode it, he was furious with disappointment at finding it not as quiet as it was warranted to be. As soon as he got back to Bedford Lodge he threw the reins to a lad, saying, 'This brute's only fit for a blooming policeman to ride! Take it up the Station Road, and give it to the first slop you see. D'ye hear? Now off you go!'

So away went £700-worth of horseflesh as a gift to what must have been an absolutely astonished member of the Suffolk constabulary. Such eccentricity, compounded of petulance and generosity, was the Squire all over.

In referring to a policeman as a slop (an abbreviation of ecilop, backslang for police), the Squire demonstrated how much better acquainted he was with the jargon of the criminal classes than ever he had been with the classics in which the Rev. Merriot had sought in vain to instruct him at Eton.

On arrival at the Limekilns, the still broader expanse of gallops across the Flat on the racecourse side of the town, faraway Choke Jade or whichever of the other working grounds they were using, the Squire would change his hack for a racehorse and have as busy a morning as any of the top-flight professional jockeys. While the Bedford Lodge horses walked round in circle after circle, three or four at a time would be taken out to go through their paces with the Squire taking a mount in every gallop, along with Jack Watts, Tommy Loates or another of the jockeys regularly associated with the stable. By breakfast time the tall, fair young man with the slightly hunched shoulders and bushy sideburns would have ridden a dozen miles, and that on a starvation diet.

Back at Bedford Lodge, the Squire would cope with whatever correspondence the morning had brought. This was a simple and undemanding task. If the season were summer, the letters went straight into the wastepaper basket. If it were winter, they were consigned to the fire. In both cases they were unopened.

Having thus summarily dealt with his correspondence, he would be off to whichever racecourse he was riding at that day. Railway journeys played a large part in the Squire's life. Somebody once estimated that the amount of money that he spent on fares during any year would have bought a freehold in Curzon Street. And, to add to the expense involved, he would frequently pay one of his associates to keep him company and amused on the journey.

While at Bedford Lodge, the Squire would make the sixty-two-mile journey to London to reach the new enclosed courses at Sandown and Kempton Parks as well as other meetings at Epsom and Windsor and the now long-defunct ones at Hampton and Croydon. The only course at which he could ride within comfortable driving distance of a horse-drawn vehicle from Newmarket was Huntingdon, where there was just one meeting on the flat each year: a two-day affair in late August or early September, at which the Squire generally made the best of the opportunities offered. He rode his first winner at Huntingdon on Tommy Upton, who beat his only rival without being out of a canter in 1887.

To reach meetings further afield than Huntingdon, the Squire and the rest of the Newmarket contingent caught the train at the town's old station, disused these many years though still standing and today regarded as an important example of Victorian architecture. Much to the chagrin and exasperation of Martin Gurry, a stickler for proprieties, the Squire generally left him to his own devices throughout the journey and, instead of discussing plans for the riding of the day's runners, would go to the back of the train to play cards with the lads in the horsebox, where he could savour to the full the latest dirty stories being passed round the yards. On being asked by the indignant Gurry why he usually travelled with the lads, the Squire replied quite simply, 'They amuse me.'

On the whole, though, the Squire was anything but languid in the expression of his sentiments. One of the most appalling scenes he ever made was after he had been beaten on Grand Composer in the Shepperton Welter Handicap at Kempton Park in 1887. As he had looked like being given a walk-over, he told Charlie Morton, who was then training for him at Bedford Lodge, to find an owner willing to provide some opposition to Grand Composer, even if it meant paying for it. Eventually Morton managed to persuade Tom Stevens Junior to start Country Boy in consideration of £100 of the Squire's money. The bookmakers, however, did not share his confidence in Grand Composer and asked for 11/8 about Country Boy, who, with Tom Cannon putting up a pound overweight, beat Grand Composer ten lengths, thereby earning Mr Stevens £101 on top of the £100 he had been paid by the rider of the loser just for running!

The Squire went absolutely livid with rage. There he was, beaten to the wide after having paid all but the full value of the race for what he had fondly thought was just token opposition. As he brought Grand Composer back to the unsaddling enclosure, he treated all within earshot to a vivid tirade of unadulterated obscenity that made observers wonder more than ever whether the term Gentleman Rider was altogether applicable in his case.*

Kempton Park seems to have brought out the worst in the Squire. At one of Sunbury course's Bank Holiday meetings, he rode a horse that started at 7/4 on in a field of three after its trainer, William Stevens, and his brother Tom had backed it as though defeat were out of the question. They were not to know that the Squire had carried on the libations of the previous evening throughout the morning, with the result that he was so hopelessly drunk that only by taking a close hold of the horse's head could he stay aboard, there being no possibility of his riding any sort of race. Once again the Kempton stewards proved remarkably forbearing by taking no action whatever, though more discerning, or more incensed, onlookers passed a few pertinent remarks about the disadvantages of Gentlemen Riders training on neat brandy or the advantages of a balancing pole over a whip.

*In his autobiography, Charles Morton places the above incident at Alexandra Park and says that Grand Composer was the horse that beat the Squire's mount ten lengths after his owner Billie Brown had been paid £100 to start. Charles Morton was an old man when he wrote his book. This is one of the instances in which his memory played him false, as the Squire never rode in a match at Alexandra Park while Morton was training for him, and Grand Composer never ran in a match other than that in which the Squire rode him at Kempton Park.

Having passed the scales, the Squire flung his saddle across the weighing room and then stood quite motionless, staring into an alcoholic void. Meanwhile the brothers Stevens sat in anguished silence on the bench outside the weighing room. The common characteristic of this family of large, dark-bearded men was a melancholy expression more suggestive of a long tradition as undertakers' mutes than of training racehorses. Sitting contemplating the losses sustained through the drunkenness of their millionaire patron, they looked even more lugubrious than usual. At length one of them produced a railway timetable, looked at it for a few minutes and, without breaking the deathly silence, pointed to a train. In unspoken agreement, the gloomy brethren rose to walk away at a funeral pace, the one behind the other, across the paddock to the covered way to the racecourse station.

When the Squire was away for days on end, riding in the Midlands or the North, life at Bedford Lodge went on much the same. It was hardly possible for the assembled thugs and spongers to behave much worse than they did when he was in their midst, but such room as there was for deterioration in their conduct was amply filled, as one unfortunate tradesman was to discover to his great distress.

While visiting his tailor in Bond Street, the Squire noticed how pale the man was looking, and, on making inquiries, discovered that he was recovering from a long illness and badly needed to get away to convalesce in the countryside. Reacting with characteristic sympathy and generosity, the Squire insisted that the tailor should go to Bedford Lodge for the rest he so badly needed. 'Pack up and go down this very afternoon,' said the Squire, 'and I will send a wire from Vigo Street telling my servants to treat you precisely as they would treat me.'

Arriving shortly after ten o'clock in the evening, the sickly tailor was civilly enough received by the housekeeper, but before he could reach the bed for which he longed, he was set upon by a few of the Squire's pugilistic friends, who manhandled him disgracefully, in what they thought of as good clean fun, before stripping him and carrying him upstairs. Still worse awaited the recipient of the Squire's intended kindness in the morning. Having been woken shortly after daybreak, he was made to drink a large glass of milk and brandy, the staple breakfast at Bedford Lodge, before being forced to don breeches and gaiters and sent out on to the heath to ride in a gallop.

For all his concern about the well-being of his tailor, the Squire had very little regard for that craftsman's wares, being notorious for, among many other things, the indifference with which he dressed. As often as not his neckerchief and leggings made him indistinguishable from a stable lad. Once, at Royston, he inquired of a farmer the way to the stable of Billie Brown, the owner and trainer of Grand Composer. 'Oh, it's some way from here, me'lad,' replied the good-natured farmer, 'and anyway, it's no use your going there, he's got twice as many lads as he's got horses already.' That information, though kindly imparted, was not of interest to a youth worth all of three million pounds.

The reception with which the Squire met at Bedford Lodge on his homecoming of an evening, was, of course, very different to that accorded to the tailor. If the Squire were on top of the world after having ridden a winner in the afternoon, the more needy of his house guests would improve the shining hour by soliciting a loan or payment for some purely imaginary service rendered. If, on the other hand, their patron was suffering from a famine of winners, they would endeavour to restore him to good humour by plying him with drinks and more than usually outrageous flattery before passing on to the night's revelry, be it cocking, dog-fighting or boxing.

In the large room he had built at the back of Bedford Lodge, two birds would fight to the furthest limits of courage during the last few minutes of their lives while the Squire and his riff-raff struck their bets and cheered on their doomed fancies with every kind of drunken obscenity. Alternatively, the assembled company would wallow in a real welter of blood-letting by staging a Battle Royal in which a number of birds were put into the arena to fight until there was only one survivor.

When boxing was the evening's sport, the Squire, so far as he was concerned, and it was in nobody's interests to disillusion him, played the star part. The bruisers, whom he had picked up on the racecourse or from the more disreputable London taverns, were always telling him that he could throw a heavier punch than any ordinary man, and even persuaded him that he had the makings of a champion – given the proper coaching.

The idea of the Squire being any kind of boxer, let alone a champion, was perfectly ludicrous. There was never much chance of the young man who wasted so hard to ride being able to throw a real punch. Still, the Squire wanted to learn to box and there was no shortage of tutors eager to accommodate him.

Sparring with the Squire was therefore a far greater test of the theatrical than the pugilistic art of his professional partners, as can be gathered from an account of a bout at Bedford Lodge in *Old Pink 'Un Days* by J. B. Booth, who wrote:

> At a certain state of the old brandy process of training, The Squire's opinion of his fistic capacity would rise to preposterous heights, and a turn-up with the pugilist was an inevitable demonstration. It was, of course, the pugilist's duty to flatter his patron's self-esteem, and there was the interesting spectacle of a half-intoxicated, half-lunatic millionaire feebly belabouring a professional boxer, who, puffing artistically, and simulating collapse, would gasp at intervals: 'Edge a bit, Squire! 'Edge a bit! We're on'y tappin'!'
>
> And The Squire would steady himself for a straight left, which the professional would carefully receive on a callous portion of his face, turning immediately to the crowd of trusty retainers with the anguished query:
>
> 'How long have we been at it?'
>
> Whereupon the valet Monk . . . would reply enthusiastically: 'Damn near twenty minutes!' and although the encounter had barely lasted a couple of hundred seconds, everybody was perfectly happy, and more than satisfied.

J. B. Booth was one of the ablest members of the staff of the *Sporting Times*, founded by Dr Shorthouse in 1865 and always known as the 'Pink 'Un'. As Booth did not like the Squire, it is scarcely surprising that he describes him as half-lunatic.

About the only other healthy activity in which the Squire engaged at Newmarket, beside riding work, involved his mastership of the draghounds. For a number of years up to the time of his death, he maintained his connection with the sport that had first brought him to the town by keeping the pack at his own expense, but his commitment to racing allowed him relatively few opportunities to follow it.

As well as for riding, boxing and what he was pleased to regard as the other manly sports, the Squire had a taste, of a sort, for music. Having purchased a beautifully made musical box at a long-established Bond Street shop, he horrified the cultured old man attending to his needs by demanding that the brass cylinder playing the 'Stabat Mater' be replaced by one of 'Phwat are they doin' in the name of Casey?' Lacking the Squire's breadth of taste, the directors of the firm and its highly skilled craftsmen had to admit ignorance of the latter opus. Nevertheless they assured their wealthy young customer of their best endeavours to meet his requirements and ended up having their agents scouring the United States for the elusive cylinder.

All was to no avail. The cylinder that was obtained at a cost of £500 to the Squire proved to be the wrong one. As soon as he began playing it to his cronies back at Bedford Lodge, he realized that the melody for which he had paid more than some men earned in five years was nothing at all to do with Casey. Thereupon he demonstrated his critical faculties by seizing hold of the poker and smashing the highly ornate musical box to pieces.

By and large Newmarket has always given a warm welcome to millionaires, no matter what their eccentricities and peculiarities. The Squire, however, was an exception. At the time of his arrival the town was trying desperately hard to share in the respectability of Victorian England. The last person Newmarket wanted as a resident in those circumstances was the black sheep of the Baird family, no matter how much he was willing to spend on racing.

Nobody had done more to mould the town to the times than the Scottish trainers. As well as Mat Dawson, the doyen of his profession at Heath House, there was his brother, John, at Warren House, the latter's son and namesake at St Albans, Jimmy Waugh at Meynell House, and Jimmy Ryan, who trained for Douglas Baird and other owners, at Green Lodge on the Severals. While it would be going too far to say that the ghost of John Knox actually stalked the heath, there can be no doubt that those God-fearing men from North of the Border exerted a very considerable influence on the social life of Newmarket and were in no small part responsible for the introduction of that element of decorum that had been so noticeably lacking from the atmosphere of the town in the doldrum years in the middle of the century and still further back in the heyday of the Regency.

One and all those Scots looked askance on their plutocratic young compatriot who revelled and roistered from morn to night in the company of every kind of reprobate and wastrel at Bedford Lodge.

6 THE SQUIRE IN TOWN

AS the atrocities of Jack the Ripper were committed in the autumn of 1888, and fear of their repetition lasted many a year, the Squire never became London's Public Enemy Number One. Nevertheless it would be unsafe to overestimate his popularity with the citizenry of England's capital.

Surrounded by his retinue of thugs and pugs, and scroungers of less violent disposition, the Squire roamed the streets and bars of London. The more he drank the more aggressive he became, while the heavy-handed flattery of his sycophants convinced him that he was entitled to do anything he pleased. Giving offence almost everywhere he went, insulting and even assaulting innocent passers-by, he was confident that the brawn of his hired fighters could save him from even the mildest retaliation. His friends, however, were never averse to pretending that retribution, in the form of criminal proceedings, was a great deal more imminent than was actually the case. They were fond of telling him that he did not know his own strength and that he had injured a man so badly that only payment of a very large sum in compensation could prevent the matter being put into the hands of the police. As he had an absolute horror of being brought before a court, and no recollection at all of what he might have done in his cups the previous evening, he used to pay up as meekly as a lamb for the concealment of purely imaginary crimes. Once they went as far as to tell him that he had killed a man. The Squire stumped up handsomely while honest tradesmen waited for the long overdue settlement of their accounts.

Sometimes different tactics paid even richer dividends. Once when the Squire was swaggering along a West End street in company with Charlie Mitchell, his principal henchman, they passed a swell.

'Hit him one, Squire,' yelled Mitchell, and the Squire, standing back, threw a punch that knocked the unsuspecting young dandy stone cold. When the police came to investigate, it was Charlie Mitchell who gave himself up and went to gaol for a fortnight. During those fourteen days he spent in prison he must have been paid a higher hourly rate than any man in the country doing an honest day's work.

In the gas-lit London that the Squire, Charlie Mitchell and the rest of the gang haunted, the popular restaurants were Limmers in George Street, off Hanover Square, the Blue Posts in Cork Street, the Bristol, opposite the house of Sam Lewis, the money-lender, in the same thoroughfare, Simpson's in the Strand, and Long's Hotel, the favourite resort of racing men where Ernest Benzon, the Jubilee Juggins, once lost £10,000 at billiards in a night. There were also a number of chop houses frequented by the men about town, the foreign restaurants around Leicester Square, and Romano's at 399 The Strand.

Almost all those establishments were the exclusive preserves of men. In those days it was almost unknown for women to dine in a public place, though chorus girls were often to be seen taking a late supper at Romano's, which was a favourite resort of actors, writers and other Bohemians until they were forced to take their pleasures elsewhere for a while in order to avoid being involved in the dreadful scenes constantly created by the Squire and his followers.

Before setting up in business on his own, Alfonso Nicolino Romano had been one of the head waiters at the Café Royal. In 1874 he invested his savings in a small fried-fish shop in the Strand, to which the deft Italian touch, and the change of name to the Café Vaudeville, brought a great improvement in the standard of cuisine and the class of clientele. In its early days, this establishment had just one central window flanked by two doors, the one leading upstairs, the other to the bar behind which lay the long, narrow restaurant known to its habitués as the 'Rifle Range'. As its popularity increased, the premises had to be expanded and the name changed again so that it was officially Romano's. The adjoining property was acquired and all three storeys of both that and the original building were brought into use with the interior decorated with the plush upholstery, heavy brocade wallpaper and ornate gilding that were the hallmarks of their era of peace, opulence and luxury.

For all the years that he spent in England, Romano, who died in 1901, never achieved more than an elementary mastery of the language. Before one Kempton Park meeting, he earnestly inquired of a customer, 'What win de Nateral Gland Bleeders Coal Stakes?' On another occasion a decorative china alligator disappeared. Addressing the hottest suspect, he said, 'You give me back my elevator, or Romano 'e take out snubbons!'

It was no softness of a Latin heart, still less a broad mind, that led Romano to extend a welcome to the Squire. The bond between them was, of course, the large standing order for wines, brandy and cigars that must have been a very valuable concession in view of the capacity of the Squire's rapacious entourage.

Lurching along the 'Rifle Range' after lunch one day, the Squire snatched a cigarette out of the mouth of the journalist Pottinger Stephens. Infuriated at having his postprandial relaxation spoilt, Stephens jumped to his feet to confront his aggressor only to find himself facing two or three tame pugilists. Like many another man in a similar situation vis-à-vis the same gentry, he reluctantly resumed his seat.

Among the witnesses of this incident was William Allison, the editor of the *St Stephen's Review*. Allison returned to his office in a state of highly indignant determination to give the fullest publicity to the behaviour of the Squire and his gang. Meanwhile the still more furious Pottinger Stephens had had a police court summons for assault served upon the Squire. The prospect of appearance in court produced, as usual, a very much meeker Squire than the one who blustered amid his bodyguard, with the result that he and Stephens rapidly compounded their differences with a large cash settlement in favour of the latter. News of the withdrawal of the summons reached the offices of the *St Stephens Review* just in time for William Allison to delete his vitriolic account of the circumstances that led to its being issued. Even if the message had arrived too late, Allison would not have cared. A surprisingly humourless man for a high Tory, he hated the Squire.

The money from the Squire would have been of far more consequence to the perennially impoverished 'Pot' Stephens than the insult for which it compensated. Henry Pottinger Stephens was a brilliant writer who had been intended to follow his uncle, Sir Henry Pottinger, into the diplomatic service until he drifted into journalism as correspondent for *The Times* while in Paris. On returning to England, he worked for Thomas Gibson Bowles on *Vanity Fair* and later became John Corlett's dramatic critic on the 'Pink 'Un'. Unable to repay £100 borrowed from his proprietor, he took ship to the United States, but before sailing wrote to Corlett saying that he had arranged for Jimmy Davies to succeed him as dramatic critic at £1 a week less than he had been receiving, so that by the end of two years the £100 would be repaid.

William Allison was fond of saying that the Squire had no redeeming point except the ability to ride fairly well on the flat. So bald a statement did him a lot less than justice. While it is true that he never for a moment regretted his lack of education or culture, and chose some really abominable friends, there was more true charity in him than in many of his detractors, who prided themselves on their respectability.

Long after they had quarrelled, the Squire received a letter from the wife of his former friend, Captain Jimmy Shaw, saying that her husband was desperately ill and penniless in Paris. The Squire's immediate reaction was to send for the most eminent doctor in London, to whom he gave a blank cheque and instructions to care for Jimmy Shaw and to bring him back to England with his health restored. The doctor earned his fee, which would have been a high one, and, thanks to the instinctive kindness of the Squire, the life of Jimmy Shaw was saved and his poor wife spared the misery of early widowhood.

Many other stories were told of the great generosity of the Squire, who had his other virtues too, notably a deep sense of loyalty. Throughout those heady, reckless, rowdy years of riding and drinking, he never for a moment wavered in his utter devotion to the mother who had loved him so well in lonely boyhood. The other objects of that intense loyalty, those who proclaimed themselves his truest friends, were, unfortunately, totally unworthy of it.

The Squire never stayed in any one house in London for very long, having addresses in Vigo Street and John Street and at No. 9 York Terrace, Regent's Park, at various times. Doubtless this metropolitan wanderlust was most appreciated by those who had been his previous neighbours, for little that he did would have enhanced the peace and quiet of his immediate vicinity. Once, for instance, he beguiled a pleasant evening by filling his drawing room with barrel organs and playing them all at the same time to find out which was the loudest. That did not endear him to many people in the neighbourhood.

Whether he was at Vigo Street, John Street or York Terrace, some of the Squire's heaviest domestic expenditure was on fresh fruit, of which he was passionately fond, possibly because it helped to keep his weight down. It was estimated that he ran up bills of about £2,000 a year with a West End fruiterer.

One evening in 1892, the Squire was dining with Sir George Chetwynd in the latter's house at 36 Curzon Street. Standing at the Park Lane end of that thoroughfare, No. 36 is a tall, narrow red-brick building with seven storeys above a ground floor, most of which is now the Qatar National Bank. Even down to this drab age, the large, well-proportioned hall, approached by a few broad stairs rising from inside the front door, retains something of the elegance of the Regency with white classical moulding embellishing amethyst-green panelling and the main staircase running down the right-hand wall as you face it.

Although a member of the Jockey Club, Sir George Chetwynd was always reliant upon successful punting to make ends meet, and at that juncture was in particularly low financial water. When the Squire expressed unqualified admiration of the surroundings as they dined, Sir George let it be known that it was all for sale at the right price. Thereupon the Squire made an offer that was far too high to be refused. The upshot was that house, and every stick of furniture, picture and ornament within it, changed hands there and then over the dinner table. After proper celebrations of a bargain so eminently satisfactory to both sides, Sir George walked out of the front door and the Squire made his way, as best he could, to the master bedroom.

Waking up to completely unfamiliar surroundings with a throbbing head that must have felt as if it held the anvils of a dozen busy blacksmiths, the Squire managed to murmur, 'Where am I?'

'At home, Squire,' replied the bruiser in attendance.

7 THE SQUIRE IN
THE COUNTRY

CONSIDERING that in all other respects his life was disorderly at best, and generally chaotic, it is surprising how well George Baird organized his race riding. The manner in which he conducted his campaign to be champion Gentleman Rider season after season in the 1880s had something of the precision of a military operation about it, his tactics being those of saturation.

In addition to having up to sixty horses at a time in his private stable at Bedford Lodge, he had about as many again spread among trainers all over the country. Therefore, as already mentioned, there was hardly a meeting at which he could not provide himself with a mount from a local stable.

The exact extent of his racing empire will never be known since so many of his horses ran in the names of other people, generally those of his trainers or their relatives, instead of his officially registered pseudonym of 'Mr Abington'.

Had the stewards of the Jockey Club been able to prove the identity of the owner of many of the horses that were entered as the property of W. G. Stevens or Tom Stevens Junior, it is probable that Mr G. A. Baird would have taken another holiday from racing. Why he should have continually run the risk of incurring the displeasure of the stewards by disguising his ownership of horses is necessarily a matter of conjecture. The most likely motive would seem to be a harmless vanity that led him to try to give the impression that recognition of his jockeyship earned him more 'outside rides' than was in fact the case.

For his provincial headquarters, the Squire rented Whittington Old Hall, some two miles south-east of Lichfield in Staffordshire. The choice of that establishment shows some discernment, as it is only about twenty miles from Meridien, the village generally regarded as the geographical centre of England, and thus within easier reach of more racecourses than almost anywhere else in the country.

At that time there was still a strong racing tradition in Staffordshire, which, at the outset of the reign of Queen Victoria, had had more courses with racing under Jockey Club rules than any other county, including Yorkshire. Many of these had closed by the time that the Squire took up residence at Whittington Old Hall, but the county still boasted such important training centres as Hednesford, where the young John Porter had learned the rudiments of his profession and Jim Dover had been head lad to Sammy Lord.

Whittington Old Hall, a lovely, mellow, three-storeyed red-brick house with four high-pitched gables above stone mullioned bay windows, was built for far more sophisticated tastes than those of the drunken riff-raff to whom the Squire set the pace. Adjoining the village of Whittington is Whittington Common, on which Lichfield races were run for more than two hundred years until the final meeting was held in September 1894, just over a year after the death of the Squire.

On the opposite side of the common from the village was the racecourse grandstand, a tall, narrow, dark red building flanked by two castellated neo-gothic towers with stone quoins. This is now the club-house of the Whittington Barracks Golf Club, and it has been considerably enlarged, though the wrought-iron railings and the iron canopy of the veranda used by Victorian racegoers are still to be seen above and behind the single-storey bar built on what was the member's lawn.

Lichfield had just one two-day meeting a year under Jockey Club rules. For a long time this was held in the week after the St Leger in mid-September but latterly it became a moveable feast, sometimes taking place as early as July and sometimes as late as October.

The Squire rode his first winner on Whittington Common on Tom Stevens Junior's Mount Pleasant, who justified odds-on favouritism in the Newbold Revel Plate on 16th September 1884, the year of his reinstatement. That was the day his filly Jenny, ridden by Fred Archer, was successful in the Grendon Juvenile Plate.

In 1885, the Squire was third in his only mount at Lichfield, and having missed the meeting in 1886 he won the Beaudesert Handicap on Mr E. B. Barnard's Governor and had two other rides there in 1887. The following year he won the Ingestre Handicap on Mr J. Newton's Kingsdene, and was placed on two of his other four mounts.

The Squire's riding was the feature of the Lichfield meeting of 1889, when he won on five mounts in succession and was runner-up on his only other. Five consecutive winners for the Squire at his home meeting were enormously popular with the small punters, who followed him blindly, knowing that they were always on a trier. The cheering with which they acclaimed his success not only left him cold, but was positively abhorrent to him. One characteristic, at least, that he shared with so many other rich men down the ages was a deep-seated dislike of seeming to court the populace.

While the patrons of the free course on Whittington Common hailed the Squire as a hero, whether he liked it or not, their fellow sportsmen, enjoying the primitive comfort of the little brick stand, took a very different view. By and large they could do very well without him and his winners. Best of all they could do without the roughs and toughs he brought with him.

Two of the winners that the Squire rode at Lichfield in 1889 were his own horses, King of Diamonds and Milesius. Another was Golden Butterfly, owned by Mr E. P. Wilson. That the Squire should have been given a fancied ride by Ted Wilson is an indication of how fully his fellow Gentlemen Riders had forgiven him his transgressions and recklessness of early youth. Wilson, it will be recalled, had been closely involved in the events that led to the Squire being warned off, having ridden the horse awarded that fateful hunters' flat race at Four Oaks Park.

Ted Wilson was born at Ilmington in Warwickshire in 1846, and died at Stratford-on-Avon in the same county in 1918. He was the outstanding amateur steeplechase jockey of his day in the Midlands and, arguably, in the country. In 1884 he won the Grand National on Voluptuary, and the following year won it again on Roquefort, while he was successful in no fewer than five of his ten mounts in the National Hunt Steeplechase.

After having carried almost all before him at Lichfield in 1889, the Squire had just three mounts there the following year, but won both the City Plate on Ashton and the High Sheriff's Plate on Secretaire. Confusion reigned for quite a time after the second race on the first day when A. J. Taylor, Tom Calder and Chadburn, the riders of the first three, were unable to draw the right weight and it looked as though the race would have to be declared void until the stewards found that about two pounds of lead had been attached to the scales while the race was being run. The perpetrators of this far from original prank, which had been played at Newmarket on Cambridgeshire day in 1863 and elsewhere on other occasions, were never brought to book. If the stewards had their suspicions that they were members of the house-party across the common at Whittington Old Hall, they would have found more than a handful of the local worthies eager to agree that such was all too probably the case.

When they were at Whittington Old Hall, the Squire and his cronies were no more willing to confine their rollicking and roistering to their own quarters than they were in London or Newmarket. The disturbance of the Victorian sabbath affording them particular delight, they would pile into his carriage with their patron on Sunday evenings and drive hell for leather into Lichfield. Clattering past the terraces of the artisans' houses on the outskirts of the city, they yelled and screamed as they went under the railway bridge and up Bird Street, at the end of which they left the landlord and guests of the George in a state of heartfelt relief as they wheeled left through the carriage arch of the Swan on the other side of the street just as that establishment was closing. There they demanded refreshment, alcoholic and abundant, making enough row and commotion to wake up any of the inhabitants who had not been sufficiently disturbed by the manner of their arrival.

The Swan has rambled along Bird Street as it has been built piecemeal over the centuries, starting from a pleasant little red-brick house, standing endways on to the street that was the Inn while Henry VIII was king. The arch through which the Squire drove, now covered in, divided the Georgian from the early Victorian parts of the building. At the end of the bar, on the left of what was the archway, is some dark, warm panelling that must have been there while the Squire and his retinue tippled and made merry in the same room.

Inevitably those responsible for the resumption of racing at Wolverhampton took a kinder view of the Squire than the patrons of the Swan at Lichfield, for he was to prove a staunch supporter of the early meetings at Dunstall Park, the first of which took place on Monday the 13th and Tuesday the 14th August in 1888. From three rides he won the Albrighton Plate by eight lengths on Sapienta, running in the name of Tom Stevens Junior on the first day as well as the Bushbury Selling Plate on W. G. Stevens's Fairy Ring on the second, and being runner-up on Tasso. He also owned The Skipper, a two-year-old on whom Sammy Loates beat the mount of his younger brother, Tommy, by a head in the Weston Plate.

Racing had taken place at Wolverhampton intermittently during the eighteenth century, and perhaps even before, but the first regular meetings under Jockey Club rules were held on a piece of reclaimed marshland known first as Hungry Leas and then, less graphically, as Broad Acres between 1825 and 1878. That land was owned by the Duke of Cleveland, and at the end of the lease was acquired by the town council as a pleasure ground to which they gave the name of West Park.

Although Lichfield, Wolverhampton, Worcester and the other Midland meetings were the Squire's happiest hunting grounds, by far the largest concentration of his horses outside Newmarket was located in what was then North Berkshire, where he had a large number with both William Stevens at the Yews, Compton, and his brother, Tom Stevens Junior, at Chilton. Judging by the frequency with which they put the Squire up on their runners, or the willingness with which they allowed his horses to be entered in their names (the latter being more probably the case), they must have made a great deal of money out of him one way or the other.

William and Tom Stevens and their brother Alfred, who managed the family's stud at Church Farm, Compton, were the sons of Tom Stevens Senior, who had moved from East Isley to Chilton in 1853. On his retirement, the Chilton stable was taken over by Tom Junior. William Stevens, who was noted for his almost inexhaustible patience in laying out horses for the big handicaps, was assistant to his father from the age of fifteen in 1858 until setting up on his own at the Yews at Compton in 1871.

Yet another of the southern stables for whom the Squire rode regularly, and almost certainly patronized, was that of James Prince at Lewes. Prince trained for Harry Heasman and Harry Roberts, who were both professional backers, and Major Harding Cox, the successful Gentleman Rider, as well as other owners.

The Squire also had an interest in the stable of a man called Wilson, who trained jumpers at Shipston-on-Stour in Warwickshire.

In the North-West of England, the Squire had horses with the Penrith trainer Bob Armstrong, who provided him with mounts at Liverpool and Manchester, thereby reinforcing the strong contingent that usually came up from Bedford Lodge for those meetings. Bob Armstrong's initial impressions of the Squire were of a man who was unusually large for a rider on the flat and possessed a very strong will. Whether it was in controlling his weight, or securing a ride in any particular race, he was always single-mindedly determined to be successful.

The first winner running in the name of Bob Armstrong that the Squire rode was Tottenham in the City Welter Plate at Worcester in October 1888. Robert Ward Armstrong, with whom the Squire was to be involved in a very disagreeable appearance before the stewards of the Jockey Club, was the second son of John William Armstrong, a native of Haltwhistle, Northumberland. John Armstrong had begun his working life as a boy in the George Hotel, Penrith, and prospered to such an extent that he was able to assume control of it three years before Bob was born in 1863. Bob Armstrong learned his horsemanship from hunting on the fellsides of Cumbria. Still only a boy when he made a name for himself as a rider at the local race meetings, he was soon able to turn professional and began training while no more than twenty in 1883. He was the father of the late Gerald Armstrong, who trained at Middleham, and Sam Armstrong, one of the most successful trainers at Newmarket until his retirement in 1972.

On the other side of the Pennines from Penrith, the Squire had horses with Tom Green at Beverley, in the East Riding of Yorkshire. A tubby little man with a florid, rather porcine face and a broad parting in short, straight hair, Tom Green had a wonderful flair for patching up horses condemned never to race again and placing selling platers on whom he bet heavily. Had he not liked a drink as much as a bet, he might have cost the bookmakers a lot of money by the time he died in 1899.

Unlike the Squire's other trainers, who would go to great lengths to please him in order to keep their boxes filled, Tom Green allowed himself the luxury of treating his millionaire patron in a distinctly offhand way, even going so far as to claim or buy Bedford Lodge horses out of sellers. He knew every bit as well as the Squire what would be the consequences of the stewards discovering the real owner of so many of the winners ridden by 'Mr Abington'.

It was therefore without any fear of reprisal that he claimed Henry George after the Squire had been beaten on him at Manchester's Whitsun meeting in 1890. Henry George had been bought in Ireland for 1,500 guineas, but the Squire took such a dislike to him that he made a present of him to Charlie Morton on the condition that he should be able to have the mount whenever the horse ran, a condition that continued to be honoured after the trainer passed him on to H. E. Tidy, the London solicitor.

On hearing that Tom Green had claimed Henry George, the Squire supposed that he had only to tell him that they wanted to have the horse back in order to restore the *status quo*. To his great surprise, though, he found that being a patron of the Beverley stable gave him absolutely no special standing in the matter. Tom Green had paid for the horse and that was the end of the matter, for no combination of blandishments, threats and persuasion could secure the return of Henry George. For all Green cared, the Squire, who was beside himself with rage at the end of the negotiations, could throw his saddle round the weighing room, jump on gold watches or do anything else he pleased.

8 WINNING THE DERBY

ONCE he had secured the lease of Bedford Lodge, the Squire's principal preoccupations in the autumn of 1886 were with finding someone to mastermind his venture into wholesale ownership and in the appointment of a suitably experienced trainer.

On the face of things, the answer to the first of those problems lay immediately to hand in the person of his landlord, Captain Machell, whose spectacular betting coups had made him the most sought-after mentor to wealthy young men aspiring to fame on the Turf. Had the Captain been agreeable to managing the Bedford Lodge stable as well as that at Bedford Cottage, there would have been serious drawbacks to the arrangement. The Squire would have appreciated that the interests of Bedford Lodge were almost bound to be subordinate to those of Bedford Cottage, where the Captain was, to a large extent, able to dictate to his existing clients so that he had almost complete control of stable policy. In the running of Bedford Lodge, on the other hand, he would have to pay a good deal of attention to the wishes of the owner of the string. In such circumstances, it would only be natural for Machell to give priority to the interests of the stable over which he exercised the greater authority. Therefore the Squire had to look further than the other side of his stable wall for an adviser.

Outside the ranks of the great public trainers like Mat Dawson, John Porter and Tom Jennings, the only men who could be compared with Captain Machell on the scores of shrewdness and knowledge of racing were Sir George Chetwynd and Robert Peck. Sir George, though a former senior steward of the Jockey Club, ran a highly successful gambling stable at Chetwynd House (now Machell Place) in virtual partnership with his jockey, Charlie Wood, in whose handicap expediency was rated about three stone above integrity. To the Squire it must have seemed that Sir George was in an even worse position than Captain Machell to give disinterested advice on the management of Bedford Lodge. Robert Peck, on the other hand, had just shed one of his heavier commitments, and though he still had his own stable, he could well be the man to be the brains behind Bedford Lodge, especially as his protégé, Martin Gurry, was looking for another stable.

Although still only forty years of age, Bob Peck already had a brilliant career as a trainer behind him. Born at Malton, where his father had had the Grove Cottage stable, he was only twenty-four when he won the Stewards Cup with Fichu. Subsequently he went to Russley Park, where Martin Gurry was his head lad, and won the Derby with Doncaster and the Oaks and the St Leger with Marie Stuart for the Bairds' old adversary, James Merry, and a second Derby, with the Duke of Westminster's Bend Or, in 1880. The following year he retired from training, almost certainly because of ill health, at the age of thirty-six.

On leaving Russley Park, Bob Peck went to Newmarket, where he managed the Beverley House stable with Jim Hopper as his trainer. He also shared the control of the Park Lodge stable, in which he had installed Martin Gurry to train the horses he owned in partnership with General Owen Williams. The outstanding horse shared by Bob Peck and General Williams was The Bard, who won each of his sixteen races as a two-year-old in 1885 and finished second to Ormonde in the Derby of 1886. At the end of 1886 the partners relinquished their interest in Park Lodge and Martin Gurry was given a contract to train at Bedford Lodge with the understanding that Bob Peck would act as adviser to the Squire.

This arrangement, not least the financial aspects of it, must have been very satisfactory to Bob Peck, who had hardly been at pains to keep his distance from the Squire. On the contrary, he had prudently cultivated the acquaintance of the young man whom he foresaw becoming the most prolific spender on the Turf by providing him with a winning mount on Poste Restante at Shrewsbury back in November 1884. The following year the Squire rode three more winners in Peck's blue jacket with orange sleeves when successful on Hungarian and Diss at Sandown Park, and on Hungarian again at Ayr.

As Martin Gurry had a strong puritanical streak in him and very little in the way of a sense of humour, he was not really the right man to be private trainer to the Squire, who was about half his age at the outset of their inevitably brief and stormy association. A native of Nottingham, Gurry had known the rigours and privation of apprenticeship in William Oates's Manor House stable at Middleham, where he had had to share the sleeping quarters of the stable dog. Although hardships endured during early life never made him sour, they left Martin Gurry with the conviction that men born to wealth and position should show appreciation of their good fortune. This being his creed, he was priggishly critical of the Squire, while positively detesting the layabouts and getabits that he picked up on the racecourse, at the ringside or in the West End.

Whenever that choice collection descended upon Bedford Lodge, they would hang around the stable yard, telling risqué stories to each other and the lads and doing everything else they could to interupt the running of an orderly establishment while airing their appalling ignorance of racing. All remonstrances by Gurry were perfectly useless. The Squire would always take the side of his house guests against his trainer.

Sometime about the early spring of 1887, the sorely tried Gurry reached the point at which he could no longer go on working in the atmosphere created by his unpredictable employer and his foul-mouthed, avaricious and invariably intoxicated associates. Thoroughly exasperated, Gurry told the Emperor that he had no clothes, or, to put it literally, told the Squire that he had no real friends, and that all they were after was his money, so that, when talking of their relationship in later life, he could always say, 'I was too straight for him.'

The Squire seems to have told Martin Gurry that if he did not like life at Bedford Lodge he had better go. Any attempts at mediation that Bob Peck may have made proved quite ineffective. Standing staunchly on his rights in law, Gurry made it plain that he was not leaving until his contract had been paid up. Meanwhile, until he received payment for the full term of it, or until its expiry, he was tolerating no more interference from the Squire's parasites in the running of the yard.

Nothing could have been easier for the Squire than to have written a cheque to rid himself of the sermonizing of Martin Gurry, but among his multitude of eccentricities was the capacity suddenly to change from spendthrift to miser. This was one of the occasions when he decided that the role of miser became him better. If Gurry therefore insisted on remaining at Bedford Lodge in the unwanted capacity of trainer, the

Squire would ensure that he had nothing to train. Accordingly he emptied the boxes at Bedford Lodge by sending all the horses to William Stevens at Compton, he and his riff-raff following in their wake to make merry, in their own peculiar way, in the royal county of Bershire. To all intents and purposes, the multi-millionaire had been sent packing, bag and baggage, out of his stable by his own private trainer!

As a result of his being in exile from his own yard, and the consequent interruption to the training and entering of his string, the Squire had to rely on the horses he had in the provincial stables and such genuine outside rides that came his way for the relatively few winners he rode in the early weeks of the 1887 season. On the opening day he won on Arthur Cooper's Luminary at Lincoln, and a few days later on Prince Rudolph, owned by the Malton trainer, William I'Anson, at Liverpool. In early April he was successful on Sir George Chetwynd's Portnellan at Nottingham, and shortly afterwards won by six lengths on Harry Heasman's happily named Libation at Epsom.

Hostilities between the Squire and Martin Gurry persisted unabated for a number of weeks, but in the middle of May 1887 some sort of reconciliation was effected. A few days later, the horses and the Squire, though perhaps not the most obnoxious of his satellites, returned to Bedford Lodge to be received by Martin Gurry, completely victorious in his intransigence.

Among the horses involved in this fiasco was the unraced three-year-old Merry Hampton, a rangy bay colt with quite a bit of quality about him. Bred by Crowther Harrison at the Cottingham stud near Beverley in Yorkshire, Merry Hampton was by Hampton out of Doll Tearsheet by Broomielaw and had been bought on the Squire's behalf for 3,100 guineas at Doncaster by his friend Tom Spence, a fellow Gentleman Rider, who was fast becoming somewhat portly.

During the time that Merry Hampton was a lodger at Compton, or even before his departure from Bedford Lodge, he was galloped well enough to raise hopes that he might win the Derby in what seemed to be a far from vintage season for three-year-olds. The Two Thousand Guineas had been won by Enterprise, trained by Jimmy Ryan for Douglas Baird. A week or two afterwards, Enterprise, a chestnut colt by Sterling, had broken down as a result of slipping up after jumping a pathway while out at exercise, and The Baron, trained by Mat Dawson in semi-retirement at Exning, had been made favourite for the Derby on the strength of his success in the Craven Stakes at Newmarket.

Having returned to the care of Martin Gurry a fortnight before the Derby, in which he was to be ridden by Jack Watts, Merry Hampton continued to please in his work. Consequently the Squire, Captain Jimmy Shaw, still his particular boon companion, Tom Spence and the rest of them went on backing their dark horse so that, despite his never having been run before, he started fourth favourite at 100/9, with The Baron still at the head of the market at 5/4 on.

Making the turn round Tattenham corner, The Baron was already under heavy pressure from Tom Cannon, and when Jack Watts sent Merry Hampton on shortly after they had turned in line for home, the race was as good as over. Although Cannon rode an uncharacteristically hard race with whip and spur, the Baron was able to make no impression on Merry Hampton, who beat him by four lengths.

As Jack Watts brought Merry Hampton back to the winner's enclosure, everybody waited to see how the *enfant terrible* of the Turf would greet the horse that had brought him the triumph many another millionaire has sought in vain for half a lifetime or more. But, to the utter amazement of those who could see him, the Squire, not generally remarkable for his reserve or unemotional nature, was lounging against the rails, taking not the slightest interest in proceedings and looking more like a day tripper who had lost two bob on the favourite than the owner of the winner.

'Dash it all, George,' cried Tom Spence, 'go and lead your horse in.' The Squire, though, remained quite unmoved by any sense of occasion, let alone gratitude to the men who had bought and ridden the horse for him. In what are ecstatic moments for the few men lucky enough to own a Derby winner, he displayed not the slightest sign of pleasure while persisting in his refusal to lead in Merry Hampton.

But as the Squire looked over the grey toppers of the crowd to see his colours carried into the winner's circle, he must have remembered the cool, not to say downright unfriendly, reception he had had from the Establishment of racing the last time a horse of his had stood in that enclosure after a classic. His Scottish pride would never have allowed him to give them a second opportunity to turn their backs on him. Moreover, he would have seen that he was in the position to kill two birds with one stone. While declining to lay himself open to being snubbed again, he could enjoy showing the Establishment that its values were not his values. Winning the Derby may have been the summit of the ambition of every member of the Jockey Club, but after the treatment he had received over

Busybody's Oaks, riding the humblest of winners had come to mean more than owning the greatest. In those days he really would rather have beaten Jack Watts by a short head in a seller up north than have the professional ride a Derby winner for him.

They must have been the glummest party that ever won the Derby. The Squire was sulking. 'Smush' Gurry had little cause for rejoicing. He had only had the colt back for a fortnight and still did not care for his owner very much. As for Jack Watts, he was the most reserved and undemonstrative of men. After he won the Derby in the royal colours on Persimmon nine years later, his face was to be quite expressionless as he was led back through the cheering crowd. Only when the trainer Dick Marsh slapped him on the thigh and said, 'Do you know you have just won the Derby for the Prince of Wales?' did he allow himself the glimmer of a smile. Winning for the Squire was therefore scarcely calulated to extract any reaction at all from him.

Ten days after the Derby, Merry Hampton was unplaced to Tenebreuse in the Grand Prix de Paris, then, at the Royal Ascot meeting of the same year of Queen Victoria's Golden Jubilee, both the Baird cousins were among the winning owners. While that would have afforded Douglas a great deal of satisfaction, it would have brought little or no compensation to the Squire for being grounded while proceedings were dominated by the professionals. On the opening day, the colours of 'Mr Abington' were worn by 'Tiny' White when winning the Gold Vase (now the Queen's Vase) on Quilp, and forty-eight hours later Douglas Baird's Bird of Freedom, ridden by Ryan's apprentice, Billy Warne, won the Gold Cup, for which his owner's other runner, St Michael, Tom Cannon up, was better fancied.

In the 1880s, there was no more racing after the Royal Meeting had come to an end on the Friday until the Tuesday of the following week when the Squire staged a successful return to the saddle by winning the first race at Hampton on Tommy Upton. His only other mount of the afternoon was Antler, on whom he was beaten a length by Attila, ridden by Roddy Owen. That was the last meeting ever held at 'Appy 'Ampton, as the Londoners called it, but three years later racing was revived at near-by Hurst Park.

While Merry Hampton was back in strong work in preparation for the St Leger in August, the Squire, moderately sober for much of the time, was at the top of his form as a race rider. Beginning with a double at Croydon on the Bank Holiday and another at Brighton three days later, he rode eight winners in all that month. At Huntingdon he won for the sixth time that season on reliable old Tommy Upton, his other successes being obtained at Kempton Park, Windsor and Leicester. His winning mount on the latter course was Pinkbasket, a chestnut filly owned and trained by Joe Cannon, who, six years later, would make what amounted to a last, desperate effort to save his life.

Riding an average of two winners a week in August would have been of more consequence to the Squire than Merry Hampton being found to have a bowed tendon shortly before the St Leger. For a day or two it seemed unlikely that the big bay would be able to run at Doncaster, but Bob Peck was adamant that there was no risk of his breaking down. News of his having met with a setback coming on top of his defeat in the Grand Prix caused the bookmakers to lay against him with some confidence, so that while the Duchess of Montrose's Eiridspord and Kilwarlin, a half-brother to Bendigo, owned by the headstrong, high-betting Lord Rodney, started joint favourites at 4/1, the Derby winner had only third call at 6/1.

Kilwarlin showed such temper in the paddock that he had to be withdrawn from the parade and accompanied to the start by Captain Machell's travelling head lad, who stood behind him with a long tom to make sure he jumped off with the rest of the field. Unfortunately the first start, to which Kilwarlin was well away, was a false one, and the second time the flag fell he stood stock still, impervious to the cracking whip behind his quarters, and declined to set off until the others had covered the best part of 150 yards. As none of the other jockeys wanted to make running, Jack Watts reluctantly sent Merry Hampton to the front to set a moderate pace, thereby playing right into the hands of Jack Robinson on Kilwarlin, who was able to make up his ground so gradually that the minimum expenditure of energy was involved. Coming into the straight, Kilwarlin was actually lying second to Eiridspord, with the Duchess of Montrose's other runner Timothy third on the outside and Merry Hampton fourth. At the distance marker, Merry Hampton began his run only to be checked in it as Timothy veered over to Eiridspord. Rather than go for another opening, Jack Watts forced Merry Hampton through as Timothy rolled away again, but the advantage consolidated by Kilwarlin was too great to be cut back, and at the post he was still half a length to the good of Merry Hampton, with Timothy a head away third.

The principal beneficiaries of the triumph of Kilwarlin were the creditors of the thirty-year-old Lord Rodney. Even as the race was being run, an auctioneer was conducting a sale of Lord Rodney's effects at his Berrington Hall mansion in Herefordshire, where proceedings were brought to an abrupt halt when news of Kilwarlin having won reached the rostrum.

A few weeks later came recognition of the prominence that the Bairds were achieving on the Turf, Douglas, not the Squire, being the recipient. At a meeting of the Jockey Club on 26th October, the Wednesday of Houghton week, Douglas Baird was elected a member.

By this time Douglas's younger brother Edward was also coming to the fore, both as an owner and a Gentleman Rider. As Ned Baird was born in 1864, he never knew his father, who died in the same year. Of far stronger moral and intellectual fibre than his cousin George, Ned Baird neither succumbed to whatever difficulties he may have experienced through lack of paternal influence nor showed any signs of becoming a spoiled youngest child. On the contrary, he enjoyed great popularity at Eton, where he excelled at games, particularly Fives. After Sandhurst he was commissioned in the 10th Hussars in February 1885 and joined Major Roddy Owen, Captain Wenty Hope-Johnstone, Captain Percy Bewicke and others in the select group of soldier riders who played such an important part in steeplechasing in that era. His horsemanship also made him a more than competent polo player, so that he was in the 10th Hussar team that won the Inter-Regimental tournament in both 1886 and 1889.

Like the Squire, Ned Baird soon became a patron of the Danebury stable of Tom Cannon, who trained Playfair to win the Grand National for him in 1888. Thus within twelve months one grandson of the once penniless crofter had owned the winners of the Two Thousand Guineas and the Gold Cup, another grandson the winner of the Derby, and a third the winner of the Grand National.

Playfair, on whom Ned Baird himself won several steeplechases, was a half-bred hunter by Ripponden, a stallion kept by the Duke of Rutland for his tenants, out of an unknown mare. He was ridden by George Mawson at Liverpool, where he was more than a little lucky. Frigate and Usna, the favourite, were well clear when the latter dislocated a shoulder and carried out Frigate at the canal turn. As a result, Frigate lost very much more than the ten lengths by which Playfair was to beat her.

Meanwhile the Squire was back in trouble of his own making at Bedford Lodge, where he was on worse terms than ever with his trainer. Having, like Charles II, no wish to 'go on his travels again', he adopted the opposite tactics to those that he had done the previous year and peremptorily dismissed Gurry from his service, thereby incurring the liability to pay Gurry his salary for the unexpired period of the contract. Martin Gurry was delighted. Freed from more than a year of martyrdom, he was determined to have every penny due to him, even if he had to take the Squire to court to get it.

The last thing that carried any weight with the Squire was the fact of Gurry having made him leading owner of 1887. Champion Gentleman Rider was a title he bore with pride; leading owner was not. All the same, thanks to Merry Hampton and twenty-one other horses that actually ran in his own name, Mr Abington was at the head of the list, with forty-six races to his credit. The most prolific contributor to that total was the former selling plater Tommy Upton, which had been successful nine times. When one designates Tommy Upton a former selling plater this is not to infer that he had come up in the world from the lowly status enjoyed by such a horse today. Because of the prevalence of sellers and optional sellers in the Victorian era these races were often contested by useful horses, and sometimes by good ones. It was an optional seller in which the previous year's Derby winner Blue Gown beat the previous year's Oaks winner Formosa by a head at the Epsom spring meeting of 1869. Needless to say, neither was entered to be sold.

9 ENTER CHARLIE MORTON

HAVING parted company with the censorious Martin Gurry, the Squire began to caste around desperately for a new trainer. For the moment he was left high and dry with a yardful of horses to ride and nobody to train them for him.

It was quite clear that none of his friends who had been only too free with their advice to Gurry were capable of running a stable of sixty horses, even on an unlimited budget. What also became clear before very long was that the Squire was regarded as being far from the ideal employer by the men who did have the necessary ability.

Private trainers were no longer the upper servants they had been during the early and middle years of the century. They expected to be, and in most cases were, left with a free hand in the management of the stable once running plans had been made. Subsequent meddling by the owner was much resented, while interference by the most well-meaning of his friends, let alone the variety favoured by the Squire, was nothing more than an unacceptable reflection on professional ability. As the whole racing world knew that Bedford Lodge had become an alcoholic rough-house that might have been better called Bedlam Lodge, it was inevitable that the Squire should be hard put to it to find a successor to Martin Gurry.

It was also public knowledge that the Squire did not treat his trainer with the almost unlimited tolerance and forbearance he showed to the ladies and gentlemen in his immediate social circle. On the contrary, he was the most demanding of employers. Never inclined to give serious consideration to the reasons for any of his horses being beaten, he was always impatient for success. He could never have enough winners, and the more that were owner-ridden the better. If the stable were out of form or out of luck, he would express his dissatisfaction to his trainer with considerable vehemence. Although completely indifferent to how much money he managed to throw away in other directions, he would begin to play the niggard by complaining about how much his racing cost him.

Those approached to take over the Bedford Lodge yard included Charles Morton, then thirty-three years of age and training in a small way at Wantage. As well as being an excellent stableman with great skill in placing his horses, he had something special to recommend him to the Squire, which took the form of the recognition he had given the young millionaire as a race rider.

Among the horses that Morton had at Wantage was the three-year-old Bismarck, a topically named brown colt by Pride of Prussia belonging to Arthur Cooper, a professional backer. Like the statesman after whom he was named, Bismarck was not to be trusted. In fact he was an utter rogue, a real Morning Glory if ever there was one.

Bismarck had been bought in Ireland shortly after he had won at the Curragh as a two-year-old in 1887. As Morton reckoned that he had three stone in hand of the rest of the field for the Egmont Nursery at the Epsom autumn meeting, the stable backed him down to 11/8 favourite only to see him beaten into third place.

In the spring of 1888, Bismarck was as brilliant as ever on the gallops and as exasperating on the racecourse. When hot favourite for a five furlong handicap at Croydon, he seemed certain to make amends for the shortcomings of his juvenile days as he led by ten lengths at half-way, but suddenly his courage gave out so that, in the end, it was only by three parts of a length that he scrambled home from a very moderate animal called Subduer. The badly frightened Cooper would have gladly had him shot there and then had not the more merciful counsel of Morton prevailed.

About a month later, Bismarck had 9 stone 13 pounds to carry in a welter handicap at Windsor. The day before the race the Squire, through one those intermediaries whose expensive services were always at his disposal, let it be known that he would like to ride Bismarck. There was nothing unusual about this. He would always try to cadge or buy the ride on anything for which he could do the weight if he thought there was the remotest chance of connections being agreeable. In this instance they were perfectly agreeable, for Morton had become convinced that the Archangel Gabriel could not have made an honest horse of Bismarck. Whatever heavenly guidance might or might not have achieved, the Squire had a positively electrifying effect on the colt.

Third favourite at 4/1 in a field of six, Bismarck broke so fast that everybody thought it a false start, and then went right away to win by eight lengths. Why Bismarck should have shown his form for the Squire after having declined to do so for five different professional jockeys since leaving Ireland was never explained. Possibly the handling of a heavier rider gave him confidence. In no fewer than six of his previous races in England he carried 7 stone 7 pounds or less, whereas the Squire rode him at almost two and a half stone more.

Even more elated than usual at having won a race, the Squire was convinced he had just ridden a champion sprinter. 'Can I ride him again?' he asked.

'Certainly,' replied the thoroughly bemused Morton.

However well disposed to him the Squire might have felt after winning on Bismarck, Charlie Morton was by no means keen to accept the job as private trainer at Bedford Lodge. His first reaction was to tell the man who came to him on the Squire's behalf that he preferred to remain at Wantage. To try to persuade him, the envoy pointed out that he would be working for one of the richest men in the kingdom, but the self-sufficient Morton replied, 'I don't care. These millionaires aren't altogether to my liking.'

Two months later, in the early summer of 1888, Charlie Morton was approached by the Squire's man again. He was to have any contract he wished and spend whatever he liked on buying horses. Still he demurred, well aware of all the trouble and difficulties encountered by Martin Gurry, an older and more experienced man than himself. Arthur Cooper and Johnny O'Neill, another professional backer with horses in his stable, both urged him to accept an offer than seemed too good to be true. Eventually, another of his patrons, H. E. Tidy, a solicitor with offices in London's Sackville Street, persuaded him to take the Squire's job.

Charlie Morton had begun his career with a trainer called Balchin at Telscombe, near Brighton, but soon joined his brother in the stable of Tom Parr at Wantage. Tom Parr was one of the greatest characters as well as one of the ablest trainers of the mid-Victorian era. Once an itinerant tea trader along the south coast, he had more than once had recourse to hiding in the hayloft while his stable jockey, George Hall, treated with his creditors. Fortunately for Charlie Morton, he learned a great deal about stablecraft from old Parr, and nothing at all of his haphazard methods of conducting business.

Having agreed to take over the Squire's stable, Charlie Morton had to go to London for an interview with Weatherby's, the family firm that still provides the secretariat to the Jockey Club. Although trainers were not required to be licensed until 1905, they already had to have permission to train on the Jockey Club's own ground at Newmarket. One of the conditions on which that permission was granted was that they had no horses owned by bookmakers and professional backers, all of whom were looked upon with great disfavour by the rulers of racing in those days.

With the horses of Messrs Cooper and O'Neill unacceptable at Newmarket, the former sent Bismarck to Alfred Day who trained on what is now the steeplechase course at Fontwell Park in Sussex. After the Squire had won on him at Windsor, Bismarck had taken a new lease of life. With Sammy Loates in the saddle, he won again at Bath next time out and then again for Billy Warne at Sandown Park, so that he was more than a little fancied to extend the sequence in the Stewards' Cup.

Charlie Morton told Day that Bismarck was as fit as he would ever be and needed no more strong work before Goodwood. But, like all his family, Alf Day thought he knew better than everybody else, and, being a strong believer in giving horses plenty of work, could not resist putting Bismarck through his paces. That unnecessary work had the effect of sapping the horse's new-found confidence. Coming over the hill by himself at Goodwood, he looked set to win as he liked, but the will to win had gone again, and so violently did he swerve while leading by ten lengths a furlong out that he actually put his head over the rails and Tib got up to beat him a head. Bismarck had four more races in England, winning under the strong handling of Jack Watts at Lewes, where he nevertheless had to survive an objection for crossing, being unplaced at Derby, third in the Cambridgeshire and second in the Liverpool Autumn Cup before being exported to Buenos Aires.

Although the realistic Charlie Morton was hardly looking forward to a bed of roses at Bedford Lodge, even he cannot have foreseen the displeasure his very first winner from the yard would arouse in the young man he referred to as his 'revered employer'. The horse concerned was a two-year-old called Athlete, a black colt by Galliard, whom Tommy Loates rode to win an all-aged selling plate at Goodwood on 1st August 1888.

ABOVE: *all the fun of the fair at Epsom on Derby Day 1890* BBC HULTON PICTURE LIBRARY

BELOW: *the Royal Enclosure at Ascot was dominated by that high society which the Squire despised, just as much as it disapproved of him* MANSELL COLLECTION

ABOVE: *the late Victorian racing establishment — to most of whose members the Squire was absolute anathema — on parade in the Birdcage at Newmarket* MANSELL COLLECTION

LEFT: *the stand of what was Lichfield racecourse, now the Club House of the Whittington Barracks Golf Club. The original stand was situated between the two crenellated towers on the left. Many additions to the original building have been made in recent years*

RIGHT: *Long's Hotel, Bond Street* (MARY EVANS PICTURE LIBRARY), *and Romano's and Simpson's in the Strand* (NATIONAL BUILDINGS RECORD) *were among the Squire's favourite metropolitan haunts*

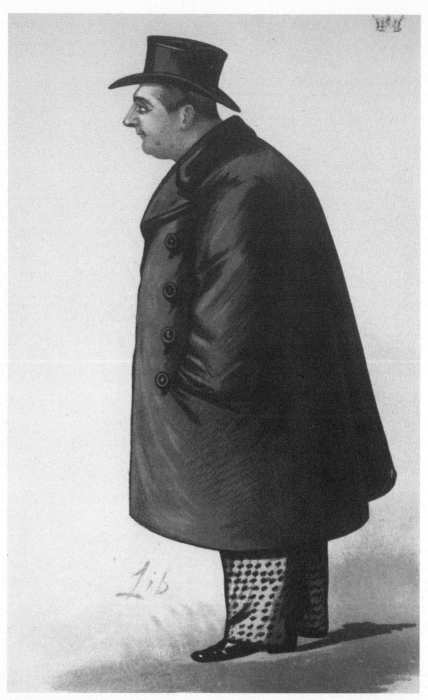

The fourth Marquess of Ailesbury, 'Billy Stomachache' to his friends, of whom the Squire was one until they quarrelled over Lady Ailesbury   BBC HULTON PICTURE LIBRARY

The winner of a selling race has to be put up for auction immediately after running, with the connections having the right to buy in. The original purpose of such events was to provide owners with opportunities to get rid of unwanted horses and to win a race at the same time. Almost inevitably, though, sellers became the media of heavy gambling. On the principal of keeping yourself in the best company and your horses in the worst, the betting stables ran horses they did not want to sell at all, backed them heavily and, if opposed at the sale, bought them in. The Squire was quite one of the worst offenders in the abuse of sellers, in which he never hesitated to run a useful horse when he wanted a big punt.

The selling price of the winner, which was the lowest bid the auctioneer could accept and all the owner could receive over and above the prize money, was advertised in the conditions of the race. Any surplus above that price was divided between the racecourse executive and the owner of the runner-up, who therefore had a vested interest in the highest possible price being made.

There was an unwritten rule that one did not bid if connections wanted the winner back and the owner of the second was usually given an inducement to make its observance worth while. But as not everybody who goes racing is quite a gentleman, the unwritten rule all too often went unhonoured. As a further refinement in the generation of ill-feeling, the rules laid down that the owner of any runner in a seller could claim any other runner except the winner on his own or anybody else's behalf for the advertised selling price of the winner and the value of the race.

When Athlete came to be put up for auction, he was knocked down to Lord Rodney, for 570 guineas. As was his wont, the Squire had absented himself from Goodwood on account of it being one of those preserves of the professional jockeys that he despised so heartily. When he learned that he had lost Athlete he was absolutely furious, notwithstanding the fact that he himself had bought the horse out of another seller at Leicester for 420 guineas the previous week and had made 150 guineas on a rapid turnover.

The Squire never much liked parting with a horse at the best of times, and losing one to Lord Rodney was like having insult added to injury. Not only did Lord Rodney own Kilwarlin, who had beaten Merry Hampton in the St Leger of the previous year, but his offence to the Squire was still worse compounded by his being a protégé of Captain Machell, who was making a habit of bidding for the Squire's platers. There was the Squire spending huge sums on the maintenance of Bedford Lodge, for which he paid Machell an enormous rent anyway, yet every time one of his horses won a seller, his ungrateful landlord, or one of his associates, bought the animal. This was in flat defiance in the unwritten rule, but then Captain Machell was not quite a gentleman and he suspected that anything good enough for the young plutocrat was, of its sort, very good indeed.

That may have been the Goodwood meeting for which the Squire took a cottage at East Dene. One of the attractions of the race week which he spent there was the match between the bantamweights Hullett and George Camp promoted by Teddy Bayly, who was to become one of the Squire's legion of secretaries. Although great secrecy was maintained about where the fight was to take place, the police found out about it and, just as the combatants were about to square up, arrived upon the scene. The cry of 'police' went up and everyone took to their heels as fast as they could. Charlie Mitchell, who was to have acted as referee, was slower into his stride than the rest, and the police, long anxious to catch him red-handed, collared him at last and marched him away.

A few days after Athlete had been sold out of that seller at Goodwood, the Squire, still nursing his resentment over the loss, complained to his trainer, 'You let that horse go and Machell bought it.'

'That's so,' replied Morton. 'He bid as much as it is worth and more.'

'I would not let him get anything of ours in the future,' said the Squire peevishly. 'If you run anything, buy it back. I don't care what it costs.'

The Monday after Goodwood, which was the first in August, the Squire, in company with thousands of holidaymakers from London and the suburbs, went to Croydon, where he had two mounts on the Great Welcomes course. On the first of these, Arthur Yates's Robertson, he was beaten half a length by Guy Mannering ridden by Arthur Nightingall of Epsom. The Squire's second mount that afternoon was Lord William Beresford's Pennant, whom he got home by three parts of a length from Queen Anne, Fred Barrett up, with Volcano half a length away third. As well as being quite close, that race must have been an extremely rough one as both the Squire and Barrett complained to the stewards about the boring and fouling of Volcano's jockey Poole, who was severely reprimanded.

The attendance at Croydon that day would have been much greater than that at a Bank Holiday meeting at Kempton Park or Epsom at the present time. Throughout the nineteenth century, and even towards the end of it, when football was still in infancy, racing was the major spectator sport available to the public, though there was also a great deal of interest in athletics in general and pedestrianism in particular. The real popular heroes, though, were the flat-race jockeys like Archer, George Fordham and Tom Cannon, each of whom would have a large section of the public following their mounts blindly in the big races.

That the Squire should have been given rides by men of the social standing of Lord William Beresford and Arthur Yates at Croydon shows that by no means the whole of the Establishment had set its face against him. Lord William Beresford, then forty-two years of age, was the third son of the 4th Marquis of Waterford and the brother of the Prince of Wales's racing manager, Lord Marcus Beresford. He was a soldier of great distinction, and, as well as having served as military secretary to the Viceroy of India, had won the Victoria Cross by charging through the Zulu lines to rescue a wounded sergeant at the Battle of Ulundi in 1879. Arthur Yates was a country gentleman with an estate at Bishops Sutton in Hampshire, where he trained horses, mostly steeplechasers, belonging to himself and his personal friends, though, for official purposes, the trainer was his head lad, John Swatton.

Arthur Yates was one of the outstanding Gentleman Riders of the second half of the last century, and Lord William, like all his family, could ride too. Therefore both commanded the respect and admiration of the Squire, who would never have dreamed of misbehaving himself in their company. They were fellow horsemen with whom he shared a real camaraderie despite differences of age and background. In his memoirs, which were set down by Bruce Blunt, Arthur Yates said of the Squire, 'I liked him very much, but unfortunately he did not choose his friends wisely, and the results were disastrous. None of his companions, however, came with him to Bishops Sutton, for he knew that I would never have tolerated any of them, and thus I always saw the best side of his nature, which was, at bottom, very gentle and pleasant'.

In the early autumn, the Squire went to Doncaster, despite there being no chance of a ride, and saw his two-year-old Master Bill ridden by Sammy Loates win the five-furlong Glasgow Plate (now the Glasgow Nursery). He also had the dual satisfaction of Athlete running unplaced in the Juvenile Stakes and buying Prosperine II for 410 guineas after she had won the Milton Selling Stakes for Captain Machell.

The meeting would have been an even better one for the Squire had he accepted an offer from old James Smith, always known as 'Rosebery' Smith. James and his brother Sidney had been course bookmakers in a rather small way until winning over a quarter of a million pounds over the coup they brought when their horse Rosebery completed the double in the Cesarewitch and Cambridgeshire in 1876. Although he had gone to the post a maiden without a previous race on the season, Rosebery won the Cesarewitch by four lengths while Fred Archer eased him to a canter. Frantic hedging made him 4/1 favourite for the Cambridgeshire, for which he had incurred a 14-pound penalty, and with Archer claimed for Lord Falmouth's Skylark, he won by a neck in the hands of Harry Constable.

Approaching Morton in the paddock at Doncaster twelve years later, 'Rosebery' Smith said, 'Now, young fellow, I've got a horse that is going to win today. I will also tell you that he will win the Cleveland Handicap and the Portland Plate. I'm getting on in years a bit and I can't look after my horses as I should. You can have this horse for £4,000.'

It was asking a lot of the horse to bring off a treble in three handicaps at a meeting of the importance of Doncaster, and, as values stood in those days, a lot of the would-be buyer. Moreover, Charlie Morton had his own reservations as he knew that 'Rosebery' Smith was not going too well, so he advised the Squire against the deal. Even when he was putting up Tom Calder in the paddock, Smith was still trying to make Morton change his mind about the horse, a three-year-old called Goldseeker, but still Morton would not have him at that price.

A few moments later, to the undisguised horror of Morton, Goldseeker won the Doncaster Welter Plate by a dozen lengths. The following day, Wednesday, he won the Cleveland Handicap by two lengths, and then on the Thursday completed the third part of 'Rosebery' Smith's prophecy by beating Mr Harry McCalmont's Castlenock by a length in the Portland handicap.

The next week the Squire went home to Scotland for the Ayr Western Meeting, on the first day of which the Stewards' Plate was very much of a Baird family affair. Of the four runners, the favourite, Woodland, was ridden by the Squire for his cousin Douglas Baird and Sanctuary by his owner, Douglas's brother Ned. The Squire did the better, but had to give best to Pompeius, ridden by the professional Jimmy Fagan, who won by three parts of a length with Ned Baird a bad third. The Squire's only other mounts at Ayr that year were Domina Sylva and Chieftain, on whom he completed a double on the second day of the fixture.

On the following Saturday, the Squire acquired the distinction of being one of the very few amateurs to have ridden a classic winner in public when he had the mount on Douglas Baird's Enterprise in the £11,000 Lancashire Plate at Manchester. That race was the most valuable of the season, with a first prize of £10,222 that was marginally more than the £10,000 of the Eclipse Stakes and well over the £6,000 of Leicester's Portland Stakes, the £4,350 of the St Leger and the £3,675 of the Derby, and the quality of the field worthy of the prize. As well as Enterprise, who had won the Two Thousand Guineas of 1887, the twenty-four runners included the Duke of Portland's Ayrshire, who had won the Two Thousand Guineas and the Derby of that season, and Lord Calthorpe's Seabreeze, who had just augmented her success in the Oaks with another in the St Leger. As the bookmakers foresaw when offering 100/1 against Enterprise, the Squire had to be content with a subsidiary role in this exalted company when Seabreeze, ridden by W. T. 'Jack' Robinson, justified favouritism by beating Ayrshire by three parts of a length.

About six weeks later, on 31st October, the Squire rode his thirty-sixth and final winner of the season on St Dominic, owned by the professional backer Harry Heasman, in the mile-and-a-half Town Selling Plate at Brighton. If the Squire had finished winning races for the year, his horses most certainly had not. At the Liverpool autumn meeting, his three-year-old Juggler consolidated his claims to being one of the best sprinters in the country by giving Lord Feversham's Queen of the Dale a year and a stone in the Liverpool Stewards' Cup. The form looked better than ever when Queen of the Dale carried 9 stone 9 pounds, to win the Wavertree Welter Handicap, with the Squire unplaced on his own horse Melifont the following day.

At the three-day Derby fixture at the outset of the next week, no fewer than four of the Squire's horses won, Jack Watts being successful on Jezreel and Master Bill, and Sammy Loates on Maynooth and Pioneer. A two-year-old brown colt by the 1875 Derby winner Galopin, the sire of St Simon, Pioneer was running for the first time. The way in which he beat the Duke of Westminster's Prebend by three parts of a length raised hopes that he might make a classic horse in 1889.

A season that had opened so inauspiciously with the final break with Martin Gurry and worse chaos than was usual at Bedford Lodge, had ended on a surprisingly satisfactory note. Charlie Morton had found 'his revered employer' unexpectedly companionable and agreeable, despite his choice of friends, and though never the most considerate of men, as generous as any. For his part, the Squire could be content with being champion Gentleman Rider again with those thirty-six winners, and though his vast string was dominated by platers, since those were the horses that he was most likely to be able to ride himself, he did have two of obvious quality. Pioneer had the scope to become a fancied runner for the Derby, while Juggler had the makings of a champion sprinter.

10 THE GREAT YEAR

BY riding sixty-one winners under Jockey Club rules in 1889, George Baird achieved success on the flat on a scale that no other amateur had ever remotely approached on the flat.

Aged twenty-seven and still able to go on the scale at 9 stone 11 pounds, the Squire was at the very height of his powers as a race rider that year. While still favouring the waiting race taught him by Tom Cannon, he whipped powerfully overhand in a driving finish to force almost the last ounce of energy out of his mounts. There must have been times when racegoers thought they were watching a reincarnation of his old mentor, Fred Archer, whom he resembled more than ever.

Champion jockey of 1889 was little Tommy Loates, who could still go to the scale at 7 stone 1 pound. He rode 167 winners. That was a higher seasonal total than any jockey except Archer had achieved up to that time. In 1888, Fred Barrett had been champion with 108 winners. That the Squire should have been able to ride more than half as many winners as the previous season's champion, despite the limitations imposed by his weight, speaks volumes for his skill and dedication, more especially as no fewer than forty-eight of those sixty-one successes were achieved at the expense of professionals. Money can buy a lot, but not even an ironfounder's millions can purchase success of that order.

As was invariably the case until the closure of the course in 1964, the 1889 season opened in the traditional way at Lincoln, where Sammy Loates rode 'Mr Abington's' Snaplock to win the first race of the first day, Monday, 25th March. Then came the turn of the Squire himself, when he won the next event on Tom Spence's Lobster, beating Freddie Rickaby on Santa Rosalia by half a length.

On the second day, the Squire rode Chamberlain to beat Ben Loates's mount by three parts of a length in a match, and, on the third, The Rejected, to win the six-furlong Welbeck Handicap under top weight of 10 stone 10 pounds. The Rejected, who was to stand him in so much good stead later that season, was owned by Johnny O'Neill, one of the professional backers whose horses Charles Morton had not been allowed to take with him to Newmarket. Another of the winners on the third and final day of the meeting was the Squire's two-year-old Grandeur, on whom Jack Watts put up a pound overweight at 8 stone 10 pounds in the Lincoln Stakes.

At the Liverpool meeting in the second week of the season, the Squire and his horses were even further to the fore than they had been at Lincoln. He rode his six-year-old Tommy Upton to win a match for the Wallassey Welter Handicap by beating George Lambton on Going Away without being out of a canter. Jack Watts won the Hylton Handicap on Juggler, and the West Drayton Stakes on Helvellyn. In addition, the Squire added to his tally by getting Sulphur home by three parts of a length from a horse ridden by George Chaloner, and walked over on Martinet, a bloodless victory which gave him no pleasure at all. Martinet belonged to a young man about town called Ronnie Moncreiffe, whose sister was Countess of Dudley. He managed the horses of Colonel John North, the 'Nitrate King', whose knowledge of racing was in inverse proportion to the fortune he had made out of chemicals in South America.

Like Juggler, the Squire's classic hope Pioneer had trained on well since 1888. Contrary to what is the case nowadays, when Leicester tends to cater for moderate horses, the Oadby course staged one of the richest races of the season in late Victorian times. This, the £11,000 Prince of Wales Stakes, was chosen for Pioneer's first outing as a three-year-old. Although beaten a confortable two lengths by the Duke of Portland's Donovan, Pioneer was anything but disgraced as Donovan had won eleven of his thirteen races as a two-year-old, including the Middle Park and Dewhurst Plates.

About three weeks later, Donovan and Pioneer met again in the Two Thousand Guineas, for which the former was favourite at 85/40 on. The winner, however, was 25/1 outsider Enthusiast, owned by Douglas Baird. He pipped Donovan by a head, with Pioneer, showing improvement on his Leicester running, coming in to finish three parts of a length away third.

Although the Squire had now reached maturity so that he was fuller of face and figure, for all his wasting, and his long light brown sideburns were thicker than they were when Busybody had enabled him to make his spectacular return to the Turf five years earlier, he remained as fickle and wilful as only really rich men can be. Fresh evidence of this was soon to be seen in connection with Pioneer.

On his running in the Two Thousand Guineas, the colt was a moral certainty for the Kempton Park Jubilee handicap, the race inaugurated two years previously as part of the celebrations of Queen Victoria's Golden Jubilee. Consequently Charlie Seaton, who was working most of the Squire's commissions at that time, did not wait for instructions before putting a monkey (£500) on for the owner and having a good bet himself.

Unaware of his agent's prompt action, and, as likely as not, without even looking at the weights for the Kempton race, the Squire told John Corlett, the editor of the 'Pink'Un', that Pioneer would not run. All the same, the colt was not scratched, and the public, drawing its own inference as to stable intentions, stepped in to back him.

On being appraised of where his interests lay, as well as those of his commission agent and a lot of the public, the Squire refused to change his mind as he would have been perfectly entitled to do in the circumstances. He was quite adamant that the horse would not run. 'I said so to Corlett,' he declared, 'and I will not go away from my word.' And that was that. Without having given any serious thought to the placing of the horse, or even consulting his trainer, he threw away £500 along with a lot of other people's money and a very good chance of winning an important handicap into the bargain.

Having burned his own fingers with as much indifference as he had everybody else's over the Jubilee, the Squire, with merry oaf and laughter, took off for the peace of the Sussex countryside the following week. On the Wednesday he brought off a double in a couple of races that had been reduced to matches at Brighton, and then, the following day, he went to Lewes, where he rode Harry Heasman's Archer to beat Bendigo's owner 'Buck' Barclay on Throne with Sir James Duke's mount a bad third in another event for Gentleman Riders.

While the Squire was gadding about the country, riding winners anywhere between Liverpool and Lewes, in the spring of 1889 Charlie

Morton was still being harassed by intermittent sniping from their far from genial landlord, Captain Machell, almost every time one of the Bedford Lodge horses won a seller. The Squire's instructions as to how this menace should be countered were explicit enough without providing a complete answer to the problem. With the Baird millions behind him, Charlie Morton could always outbid Machell, but he still wanted to prevent the other from running him up.

The cut and thrust of betting, buying and selling was the breath of life to the bachelor captain, who set little store by human relationships. Time and again he would jeopardize friendship with people he esteemed far higher than the Squire when scenting a good bet or a profitable bit of horse coping. No wonder, therefore, he could not desist from trying to buy the Squire's platers, even if it did upset his tenant and make him complain querulously of how, 'They had always been such good friends.'

Charlie Morton may have lacked Captain Machell's obsession with proving himself cleverer than everybody else, but he was just as much the complete professional racing man and master of all the chicanery needed to play the selling plate game. By the late spring of 1889, he had determined to teach Machell a lesson.

His chance came at the Newmarket second spring meeting in the middle of May. As there was no chance of his having a mount, the Squire did not grace the proceedings with his prescence, even though he had only to cross the town from where he was tippling at Bedford Lodge to see his runners. Morton was thus left with a free hand with which to pursue his revenge.

The Squire's unraced two-year-old Scotch Earl was in a seller with Jack Watts engaged to ride. Now the trainer knew that Scotch Earl had a weakness that made him a much more suitable candidate for a selling plate than most of the horses which the Squire ran in that class. All the same, the colt did have speed, so Morton took a chance and baited his trap by putting £3,000 on Scotch Earl, who started a raging-hot favourite at 6/5 on in a field of fourteen. The colt then proceeded to beat Lady Careless, a filly owned by Machell, by a length, with Grenadine a bad third.

Scotch Earl must have seemed something really worth bidding for to the calculating mind of Machell, who, as owner of the second, was in the happy position of being entitled to half the surplus. Not only was the heavily backed colt a great deal more taking an individual than the average selling plater and a son of the great Barcaldine, but the form was good since the captain's filly had won her only previous race.

The auction turned into a more than usually protracted duel between Morton and Machell. At 1,000 guineas, wily little Morton knew that he had already gone beyond the point of twice what the horse was worth, but kept bidding as though in obedience to what everybody knew were the Squire's instructions. Then, at 1,300 guineas, fearing his adversary could be coming to his limit, he let Machell have Scotch Earl.

A few minutes later, Morton, as though crestfallen at the loss of the winner, asked Machell's trainer Jimmy Jewett, the former steeplechase jockey, why the captain always bid for the Bedford Lodge platers.

'Don't ask me,' replied Jewett, with whom Morton was on the best of personal terms. 'I can't tell you what the idea is. If I asked him he would probably tell me to mind my own business.'

On returning to Bedford Lodge, Morton found himself in a great deal more heated exchange on the same subject than that which he had had with his friend Jewett.

'You have let Machell have another horse of mine,' howled the Squire like a small boy who has had one of his many toys taken out of the nursery. 'What's the matter with him? We have always been such good friends and I spend a fortune keeping up his place.' Then, suddenly ceasing to wallow in self-pity, he added, 'I tell you what to do for the future, whenever he runs a plater, buy it if it wins and claim it if it loses.'

A few days later Morton met Jewett on the Limekilns.

'That colt was not worth the money,' said Jewett.

'What did you expect?' retorted Morton, adding maliciously, 'He's a good-looking horse.'

'Yes, but he makes a noise,' said the disgruntled Jewett, who had discovered that Scotch Earl was afflicted in the wind and heard him fighting for his breath while galloping.

'Well, whose fault is that?' asked Morton. 'I didn't ask Machell to buy him. I got into quite enough trouble with the Squire without bothering about Machell.'

To complete the discomfiture of the usually astute Machell over that particular Newmarket seller, 'Young' Tom Jennings, whose Grenadine had been third, claimed Lady Careless.

A fortnight later, Pioneer, having missed what seemed a heaven-sent chance in the Jubilee, finished unplaced to Donovan in the Derby. The Squire would not have been unduly put out. He had not ridden the horse. Jack Watts had.

The week after the Derby, the Squire went north to Lancashire to ride at the Manchester Whitsun meeting, which, along with the Whit Walks, the processions of witness, and other festivities, was part of the traditional Wakes Week in the great textile city the Victorians called Cottonopolis. At that time the races were run on the New Barns course, which was situated near Trafford Park. The going there was notoriously heavy, so that most owners and trainers complained that it was more like a bog than a racecourse. On being asked how one of her horses had run at New Barns, the Duchess of Montrose, with characteristic asperity, replied, 'It disappeared down the main drain.' Not until 1902 was the meeting transferred to Castle Irwell, where racing continued until 1963.

Manchester's Witsun meeting lasted from the Wednesday to the Saturday. During those four days, the Squire had seven mounts which yielded three winners, a second and three thirds. On the first day he won on Eversfield, finished second on Boom and third on Whistle Jacket. Eversfield was owned and trained by the high-betting Charlie Archer. He had the Ellesmere House stable, which continued to stand round the corner from the Clock Tower end of Newmarket High Street until pulled down to make way for that most unedifying necessity of modern life, a car park, some twenty years ago. As Eversfield started even money and was bought in for 270 guineas, the Squire must have made Archer a good winner over the race. The Squire's third mount of that afternoon, Whistle Jacket, belonged to twenty-five-year-old Henry Milner, an unfortunate youth whose awful fate it had been to marry the Duchess of Montrose as her third husband the previous year.

After being third on Mr F. Nickson's Tottenham, his only mount on the Thursday, the Squire brought off a double on his own horse, Brighton, and Mr J. Dooley's Ossidine on the Friday, before being third again on Tom Spence's old favourite, Lobster, on the Saturday.

Some idea of how selling races proliferated during Victorian times may be gained from the fact that, although the Whitsun meeting at New Barns was one of the most important fixture in the calender, featuring, as it did, such time-honoured events as the Manchester Cup and the Salford Borough Handicap, no fewer than eleven sellers were run during the four days. One of them, the Stockport Selling Plate, was won by Bob Peck's gelding Hungarian whom the Lambourn trainer Charles Humphreys bought for 330 guineas.

After the Manchester Whitsun meeting came Royal Ascot, where Pioneer was able to avoid a fourth clash with Donovan. The latter won the Prince of Wales Stakes on the Tuesday, leaving Pioneer to land the St James's Palace Stakes on the Thursday. Another success at Royal Ascot would have left the Squire quite unmoved. After all, it was still only another of those meetings for hired jockeys where the weights gave a chap no chance of riding his own horses.

Departing from his usual practice with regard to such fixtures, the Squire did put in an appearance at Goodwood that year – without enjoying it very much. He really hated being grounded. Walking discontentedly around the paddock with Charlie Morton, the young millionaire remarked, 'I don't care for these meetings. They don't interest me at all. I suppose you haven't got anything on which we could have a bet?'

If he could not ride, the only thing that went any way towards relieving his boredom was a heavy plunge. He loved piling £4,000 or £5,000 on a selling plater.

'Yes, I have got something good for you,' replied Morton. 'If you like to risk Sorceress in a seller, there's no doubt about her winning.'

Sorceress was an unraced two-year-old filly by Touchet out of Enchantress, and therefore full sister to Juggler. Unfortunately, one of her eyes had been knocked out by a careless stable lad, but the accident had not impaired her ability and Morton knew she was good enough to win any seller in the country. The difficulty would be in buying her back afterwards.

The Squire announced that he would have £4,000 on her, Charlie Morton added another £1,000 of his own, and John Hammond, the former stable lad who had become one of the smartest operators on the course, went off to spread the money round the ring. By the time he had finished his work, the bookmakers were asking for 100/30 Sorceress.

With Tommy Loates riding at his minimum weight of 7 stone 1 pound, the gamble duly materialized when Sorceress beat Harry Heasman's Paget by a length and a half.

As a professional backer, Harry Heasman knew the etiquette to be observed in that sort of situation. 'What about this animal?' he inquired of Morton. 'Of course, you are going to get it back?' Confirming that this was the intention, Morton asked Heasman to bid for him.

A sister to Juggler winning and backed first time out, whether or not she only had one eye, was too much of a temptation for Captain Machell. The selling price down on the card was £100, but Machell tried to clinch the matter at a stroke with an opening bid of £500 for the bay filly. To his amazement, Heasman countered with £1,000. Machell turned his cold eye to the other side of the auctioneer's rostrum to see Morton standing beside Heasman. He was up against the Squire's money again and, for all he knew, could be left with another Scotch Earl on his plate. Turning on his heel, Machell strode away as Sorceress was bought in. She won again for the Squire at the Liverpool autumn meeting of the following year, and was exported to Germany as a four-year-old in 1891.

After that incident at Goodwood it was a very long time before Captain Machell risked running one of his own horses in a seller when the Squire or his trainer was at a meeting. Only too well did he know that they would have their revenge for the £900 he had cost them over Sorceress and settle a few more old scores at the same time by claiming it.

One of the climaxes of the Squire's riding career came on Saturday, 7th September 1889, when he forced a dead-heat with no less a formidable adversary than Jack Watts at the end of the mile of the Olympian Welter Handicap at Sandown Park. He was riding Tom Cannon's chestnut six-year-old True Blue II, and Watts was on Easington, who was receiving 25 pounds. Freddie Rickaby was a bad third on Violante. There was no deciding heat, and the stakes were divided. An interesting condition of that race, and one quite common at the time, was the free entry for 10 guineas members of the Sandown Park Club. Entry for horses belonging to non-members cost 3 guineas.

Later in September, the Squire gave Newmarket, the West End and his other haunts in England a respite from his raucous revelry by returning north to his own country to ride at the Ayr Western Meeting. So far as the yield of winners was concerned, the outcome of this expedition was eminently satisfactory to the Squire. How much his dour compatriots enjoyed the pleasure of his company, and that of the carefully chosen coterie he brought with him, must be open to question. The gentry, however, gave him the only welcome he wanted by providing him with mounts to supplement those that he had brought with him from the South.

Of the eight races in which the Squire rode at Ayr that year, he won six, three of them on Johnny O'Neill's old faithful, The Rejected, who was to go on to still greater things by winning the Lincolnshire in the hands of Freddie Rickaby the following season. On the opening day, the Wednesday, he brought off a double on Mr S. Platt's The Solent and Mr C. J. Cunningham's Blair Hope. On the latter, he beat his cousin by marriage, 'Bay' Middleton, on Dazzle in the Stewards' Plate, a handicap in which horses ridden by professionals had to carry 5-pound penalties. Blair Hope's owner, Charlie Cunningham, whose home was Muirhouseland, Kelso, just a few miles from Stichil, was a well-known cross-country rider in the Border country and beyond, though he was a well-built man of more than six feet in height. Earlier that year, he had been second in the Grand National on Why Not, while in the season of 1882–3 he had been champion amateur steeplechase jockey with forty-seven winners from a hundred mounts. He continued to play a leading part in steeplechasing in the North, as owner and steward, until his death at the early age of fifty-six in 1906.

On the second day of the Western meeting, the Squire finished fourth of five on Flumen, owned by the young Duke of Montrose, and then brought off another double on Belfry and The Rejected. His appearance on the back of Belfry would have raised a few eyebrows, as he was wearing the blue and orange colours of his recently departed trainer, Martin Gurry, with whom he still had substantial financial differences outstanding.

The Squire made a bad start to the final day by falling on the odds-on favourite Happy Thought in the first race. The tumble can have done him no harm since he went on to bring off his third double of the meeting by winning both the Consolation Welter Plate and the Land of Burns Plate on The Rejected. The same afternoon, the Duke of Montrose's Dazzle, whom he had beaten on Blair Hope two days earlier, won the Ayr Gold Cup.

The following month Juggler, Jack Watts up, won the Liverpool Autumn Cup for the second year running by giving Ronnie Moncreiffe's Sea Song 2 stone and a beating of two lengths. Two days later, Freemason, another of the Squire's horses, won the Liverpool St Leger. Juggler had one more outing in 1889, providing the Squire with a winning mount when odds-on favourite for a small race at Warwick.

Juggler was the Squire's sixtieth winner of the season, but only the thirteenth to have run in his own name. Of the other forty-seven, not a few, including those running in the names of the Stevens brothers and cunning old Tom Green of Beverley, were, of course, his property. Quite a number of his genuine outside rides were given him by trainers, like Charlie Archer, in the hope that he would show his appreciation by sending a few horses into their yard. Other outside rides came as a result of anything from a hint in the right quarter or just barefaced cadging to the use of the power of the purse. There was simply no limit to what

George Baird would pay if he thought he was going to throw his leg over a winner.

The way he came to ride the last of his sixty-one winners in 1889 was typical of his method of operation once he had set his heart on a particular mount.

The Lambourn trainer, Charlie Humphreys, who had bought Hungarian out of a seller at the Manchester Whitsun meeting, had that old gelding in another such event on the second of the three days of the Manchester November meeting, the closing fixture of the season. Although Hungarian, a son of the Hungarian-bred Derby winner Kisber, had not run since being acquired by Humphreys, five months previously, he was regarded as having a very good chance of winning again.

Nobody appreciated Hungarian's chance better than the Squire, who had ridden him to win at both Sandown Park and Ayr back in 1885. He asked Morton if he could get him the ride.

'It might be done,' replied the long-suffering Morton, who was thereupon dispatched to fix things up with Humphreys.

'Well, I don't know,' said Humphreys dubiously. 'I have engaged Fred Webb to ride him, and I don't see how you can get him off.'

'Oh, that's easy enough,' countered Morton, who was well used to touting for rides for his employer. 'Fred knows the Squire. He won't mind.' That was true, Webb had won a number of races for the Squire from time to time including the Fern Hill Stakes, then run at the Royal meeting, and three other events on Necromancer in 1885.

'All right,' agreed Humphreys. 'If you can square Webb, I don't mind. But I shall want him to put me £200 on it.' These not undemanding terms having been agreed upon, the Squire duly rode Hungarian, who showed what a good thing he had been by winning by three parts of a length pulling up.

As was so often the case, the Squire promptly forgot about the obligations into which he had entered, not because he wanted to get out of them, but because he rarely gave a thought to the business side of life whether in connection with paying his wine merchant or making things right with a jockey over a ride. In this case he had even forgotten to back Hungarian. Therefore he had to pay Charlie Humphreys £800, that being the £200 on at starting price, and another £200 to Fred Webb for standing down. But even £1,000 for a ride did not worry the Squire in his heyday so long as it was a winning one.

If the Squire's feat of riding sixty-one winners under Jockey Club rules in 1889 was remarkable by comparison with the achievements of the professionals, it was little less than staggering when set against those of his fellow Gentleman Riders. Whereas he headed the list for 1889 with those sixty-one winners, Willie Moore, who was second, rode just three, third place being shared by Arthur Coventry, Mr R. Woodland and Mr J. Craig with two winners apiece.

Another fifteen amateurs, including George Lambton, 'Buck' Barclay, Charlie Cunningham and Harding Cox, rode one winner each. That means that the rest of the amateurs enjoyed twenty-four successes between them, so the Squire rode more than twice as many winners as all the rest put together.

11 BILLY STOMACHACHE
AND DOLLY TESTER

IF the Squire ever had a friend of wealth anything like comparable to his own, that friend, for a time at any rate, was George William Thomas Brudenell-Bruce, Lord Savernake, later Marquess of Ailesbury. This was the nobleman known to his despairing family as 'Dear Willy' and to everyone else as 'Billy Stomachache' – in rhyming slang for Savernake rather than in allusion to an unsatisfactory digestive system. His digestion may have been the only satisfactory thing about him.

The Brudenell-Bruces were descended from Sir Thomas Brudenell, a staunch supporter of the Royalist cause in the Civil War, and were originally a cadet branch of the family of the Earls of Cardigan, whose title they inherited on the death without issue in 1868 of that same Lord Cardigan who had led the charge of the Light Brigade. The 2nd Marquess of Ailesbury had enjoyed some success as a racehorse owner after having shown commendable perspicacity by becoming the first patron of the Fyfield stable of Alec Taylor Snr. It was for him that 'Grim Old Alec' trained St Albans to win the St Leger in 1860.

On the death of the 2nd Marquess of Ailesbury in 1878, the title passed to his brother Ernest, who had been Member of Parliament for Marlborough over the previous fifty years. He was married to Louisa, the elder sister of the awesome Caroline, Duchess of Montrose, and though he made no lasting mark as a parliamentarian, he served his country to the best of his ability. The same could hardly be said of his eldest son, George Brudenell-Bruce, who achieved the limited military distinction of being a lieutenant in the 14th Hussars. Rather than make any serious attempt to follow the soldier's trade, he devoted himself to the pleasures of the flesh and the bottle with such success that his health was seriously undermined. Seeking rest and recuperation in the warmer climate of Corsica, he went to Ajaccio, where he died at the age of twenty-nine on 28th May 1868. He was survived by his sorely tried widow Evelyn, daughter of the 2nd Earl of Craven, their son, Billy Stomachache, and a two-year-old-daughter, Mabel, who was destined to bring fresh honour to the great house of Brudenell-Bruce by her marriage to Bob Sievier, the owner of Sceptre. Therefore, when old Lord Ailesbury died at the age of seventy-five on 18th October 1886, his titles and estates passed to his twenty-three-year-old grandson.

The 4th Marquess of Ailesbury was one of those unfortunate individuals who contrive to be as ridiculous as they are pathetic and had already made it plain that he was going to be an infinitely greater source of embarrassment to his family than ever his father had been.

Having run away from Eton after refusing to be thrashed for impertinence to the headmaster, Billy Stomachache had set about spending money with absurd recklessness and running up bills without any regard for the manner of their settlement, until, in desperation, he had to turn to Sam Lewis, the fashionable Cork Street money-lender.

Although Billy Stomachache came from the landed aristrocracy and the Squire from the plutocracy of the Industrial Revolution, they had a good deal in common. For one thing, they were much of an age, Billy having been born on 18th June 1863, some eighteen months after the Squire, and then, again, both had been left fatherless before adolescence and brought up by devoted mothers in the remote countryside with only grooms and other servants for companions. Both left Eton in highly discreditable circumstances, and both thereafter sought their friends among the flatcatchers and other obsequious parasites who haunted the West End and the racecourses.

Finally, both were warned off. Here, though, the similarity between them ends. Whereas the Squire was a highly successful Gentleman Rider, Billy Stomachache was no more than a failure as a punter. Worse still, he deteriorated so far as to allow himself to be used as a figurehead in a piece of flagrant villainy, whereas the Squire, on reinstatement, always rode and ran his horses fairly, even though he did continually break the rules of racing by entering them in the names of other people.

Surrounded by a gang of unprepossessing spongers and a selection of assorted toughs, Billy Stomachache divided his time between the attendance at race meetings and lounging around London, throwing his weight about inexcusably and being throughly offensive to everybody. Great Aunt Caroline, Duchess of Montrose, his father's brothers, Lord Frederick and Lord Henry Brudenell-Bruce, and the rest of the family were appalled and bitterly ashamed. Dear Willie was turning out a dreadful disappointment.

In appearance he was a puffy, portly youth with a heavy jowl and a prominent nose that was almost an extension of the straight line of his receding forehead. For some reason that he never saw fit to explain, he was wont to dress as though trying to look like a cabman or omnibus driver. His outer garment was usually a heavy box-coat, of the variety worn by coachmen in the early years of the century, while in the way of headgear he favoured a hard black hat with a low flat crown. On that extraordinary coat were real half-crowns instead of buttons. When his career on the Turf was drawing to its disastrous close, a punter, down on his luck, tried to touch him for a loan at Kempton Park. 'You want to borrow half a crown?' exclaimed the Marquess, then, pointing to his coat, 'Don't you know the only half-crowns I have nowadays are these?'

In keeping with his efforts to look like a cabby, Billy Stomachache considered himself a great authority on the art of driving and was never slow in his criticism of how others handled the reins. With that sense of humour that was entirely his own, and in the rustic accent he liked to affect, he would cry out, 'I say, guv'nor, who feeds the pigs when you be driving?'

About the only thing that he did have in common with the cabbies was a really remarkable command of the vernacular. Running around the farms and stables of the family property in Wiltshire during boyhood, he had acquired a wide knowledge of terminology denoting procreation and other natural functions as well of expressions of simple annoyance. Having enlarged that carefully cultivated vocabulary in the unsavoury society he kept in London, he was so much the master of the infelicitous phrase that he had no need to repeat himself for ten minutes at a time when he 'rapped it out'.

He loved to pose as the strong, aggressive extrovert. While being fitted out with his peer's robes, he instructed the tailor to sew two large pockets in the skirts.

'Whatever for, m'Lord?' asked the tailor.

'For bags of flour, old sport,' replied Billy Stomachache. 'The very first time the Lord Chancellor hands me any of his lip he's going to "get the miller".'

Such empty bravado was typical. Having acquired his robes, the next thing he had to do was to embark upon the more serious business of selling off the Brudenell-Bruce's Yorkshire estates to meet debts of something in the order of £200,000.

Before becoming marquess, Billy Stomachache had entered into both the ownership of racehorses and matrimony. As his trainer he selected J. B. Tyler, a man, unfortunately, of highly developed criminal instincts, but in his choice of wife he showed a measure of surprisingly good taste by marrying the actress Dolly Tester. That lady had been born Dorothy Julia, daughter of a Mr Thomas Haseley of Brighton. She was a most attractive person, dainty and graceful, and endowed with quite anough intelligence to appreciate the desperate need for her husband to mend his ways. It was, of course, a dreadful misalliance. Even his family admitted that she was far too good for him.

During the early days of his marriage, Billy Stomachache, or the Marquess of Ducks as he was now dubbed by the 'Pink 'Un', was inordinately fond of his pretty, pert young wife, and, being of a jealous disposition, quickly offended when anyone took what he considered liberties with her. While they were dining with Sam Lewis in Cork Street one evening, a rather flashy young captain became extremely generous with his compliments to Lady Ailesbury. To show his displeasure, her Billy poured the contents of the soup tureen down the soldier's back.

In due course Billy's ardour waned, or, more probably, his monstrous behaviour made it impossible for Dolly to reciprocate any affection that he might have felt for her. Whatever the case may have been, she was soon looking for an improvement on the company of her husband, who had added to his infamy by getting warned off, and jumping straight out of the fire into the frying pan she embarked upon an affair with the Squire.

Common tastes, the extreme disfavour with which the Establishment looked upon each of them and the frequency with which they met on the racecourse combined for a short time to make close friends of George Baird and the Marquess of Ailesbury. They often dined together, and on such occasions Billy had no need to be ashamed of his predilection for pouring soup over people or otherwise misusing the victuals. Once, when they sat at table with a large gathering of their cronies, male and female, all sense of decorum vanished even more quickly than usual. As the party became rowdier, food flew all over the place until a chicken, from the direction of Billy, hit the Squire.

'Here, I say, Ducks,' protested the Squire, 'that's a bloody sight too much.'

'Oh no,' retorted the Marquess, anxious to show he knew the niceties to be observed in such society. 'I swear I have only been throwing jellies.'

Having decided that there was more fun to be had in the retinue of the Squire than in putting up with the boorishness of her husband, Dolly made herself available to act as hostess at the former's house-parties. In opting for the Squire, she gained at least one discernible advantage. Billy never knew where the next penny was coming from, or, rather, he knew very well that it was coming from Sam Lewis though he did not know the rate of interest. The Squire, on the other hand, had both a fortune and a generous nature.

One year, it was either 1887 or 1888, the Squire departed from his practice of ignoring the Royal Meeting on account of its failure to cater for Gentleman Riders, and rented a house in the Ascot area. In the middle of the week he decided to show his appreciation of services rendered by Dolly by wiring to a West End jeweller to send down a selection of his wares from which she might take her pick. The same evening they had one of those tiffs that were part and parcel of any woman's life with the Squire. When the jeweller's man arrived with his trays of bracelets, rings and brooches while the Squire was out the following day, Dolly took her revenge by choosing the most expensive item for herself and distributing the remainder of the trinkets among members of the party still present. Having done so, she prudently packed her bags and took her leave immediately. Returning to find a jeweller's bill for £10,000 and not even a note of explanation for Dolly's abrupt departure, the Squire flew into a fearful rage, giving voice to a flood of fine language that even Billy Stomachache might have grudgingly admired.

The Squire, had he been of a philosophical turn of mind, might have consoled himself with the thought that other women had served him worse and contrived to make him look even more ridiculous. There was, for instance, the wife of a well-known racing character to whom he gave a cheque for £100,000 in the expectation of her fulfilling her promise to elope with him. Upon the lady presenting it at the bank and asking for cash, she was informed that the Squire's personal authorization would be needed before so large an amount could be paid. Agreeing that this was perfectly reasonable, she sat down while a clerk was sent to the Squire, who confirmed the validity of the cheque. The lady then drew the money, went straight back to her husband, with whom she shared it, and thereafter never spoke to the Squire again.

The Squire tried desperately hard to get his money back, but finding he had no redress in law or anywhere else, determined to take the matter into his own hands. When Christmas came he sent his ertswhile hearthrob a parcel accompanied by a note that read, 'Although you have treated me so badly, I am always thinking of you. I am sending you something which I hope will bring you luck.'

Thinking the pitcher had been brought to the well for her yet again, the avaricious one tore open the package. And found a dead cat with its throat slit. The Squire loved his little jokes.

Possibly solely on account of that incident at the Ascot house-party, though he probably had other grievances, real or imaginary, against her, the Squire resolved to settle his score with Dolly Ailesbury. The vindictiveness he displayed in this instance was untypical of him, as he decided to have her ladyship kidnapped and held prisoner at his pleasure. In his search for somebody to undertake this enterprise, he did not have to look beyond the very unselect circle of his most intimate companions. Among these was a man called Riley, who was quite ready to indulge in a little abduction at the right price.

Riley is necessarily a shadowy figure since nobody found it worth leaving any record of him in diary or memoir. It would seem that he was an ex-soldier come down in the world. He had seen some service in India and had, while riding over hurdles, acquired a reputation for the regularity with which he fell off rather than that with which he won.

In the May of 1889, Lord and Lady Ailesbury were in residence in a large house in the vicinity of Maidenhead, to which Riley secured an invitation. A day or two after his arrival, he effected the removal of his hostess, probably on the pretext of taking her for a drive, and carried her off to rooms in Southsea, a suburb of Portsmouth.

After a fortnight's incarceration, Dolly managed to persuade Riley that there would be no harm in his taking her to the pony races held at near-by Grange Port. That meeting was under the management of Major 'Treasure' Dalbiac, a contributor to *Country Life* and other sporting publications until his death at Senekal in the Boer War.

Whether from a letter sent by Dolly without the knowledge of her gaoler or by another means, Billy Stomachache learned of their intention to go to the ponies. Despite the fact that his being warned off made him as much a disqualified person at such a meeting as one under Jockey Club rules, he made his way to Grange Port with the intention of retrieving his wife.

For once he was completely successful, though, as in anything else he undertook, it was in an atmosphere of unadulterated farce. When he and Riley came upon each other behind the stands while a race was being run, high words were followed by blows. The ensuing exchange was some way from being ferocious, as no two opponents could have been more evenly matched on the score of ineptitude. Billy Stomachache was no more noted for his courage than he had been when declining to be thrashed at Eton, while Riley, for all his military background, was no man of valour. As they were belabouring each other ineffectually Dolly reappeared from the ladies' cloakroom and set about the pair of them with her parasol until Major Dalbiac, having been apprised of trouble afoot, appeared on the scene and put an end to these half-hearted hostilities.

The marquess then bore off his lady wife in what was as near to triumph as he had ever been. Riley, after a restorative drink, returned to explain to the Squire as best he could how he had managed to lose his prisoner. Passing a bookstall on his way through Portsmouth, his eye was caught by a novelette. Its title, *Dolly: a Love Story*, did nothing to amuse the unsuccessful kidnapper.

By the time he had paid Riley for the risks involved in this flagrant piece of villainy, paid the rent for the rooms in Southsea and the other overheads involved, the whole enterprise was estimated to have cost the Squire £50,000.

12 GALLINULE

BY far the most important horse ever owned or ridden by George Baird was Gallinule, sire of the incomparable Pretty Polly.

Gallinule was a chestnut with a neck like a bull in exact proportion to his massive girth, and markings that can only have endeared him to the touts who surreptitiously watched the gallops on Newmarket Heath. As well as long socks on his hind legs, shorter ones on his forelegs and a broad blaze, he had a white patch shaped like an hour-glass running up from the nostril on the near side of his face.

Bred in Lincolnshire by Mr J. C. Hill in 1884, Gallinule was by Isonomy out of Moorhen by Hermit, winner of the sensational Derby of 1867. He was therefore two years older than his half-brother Pioneer, who, as mentioned earlier, won at Royal Ascot and was placed in the Two Thousand Guineas while owned by the Squire.

Gallinule carried the colours of Mr E. H. Wood when unplaced first time out at Leicester in early April 1886. On Mr Wood dying shortly afterwards, the big chestnut was acquired by the Squire's good friend Lord Savernake, who sent him to his rascally though very skilful trainer J. B. Tyler. That dubious individual and the unscrupulous gamblers who patronized his stable, had been quick to see the advantage of an association with a young man of title, who could be manipulated for their own ends with the greatest of ease.

Soon after being unplaced first time out, Gallinule showed enough improvement to raise hopes of his being top class. On his second appearance, he carried Billy Stomachache's colours successfully in the Queen Elizabeth Stakes at Kempton Park. He also won the National Breeders Produce Stakes (now the National Stakes) and another race at Sandown Park, and was runner-up on two of his other four appearances during his first season.

By the time that he was next seen in public, Gallinule had developed a serious defect. He had begun to break blood vessels, a weakness that may have been inherited from his maternal grandsire Hermit. As a result he became so hard to train that he could only be lightly raced as a three-year-old. After being unplaced at Leicester in the first of his three races at that age, Gallinule took part in the inaugural race for the Jubilee Handicap at Kempton Park, where he was the only one of the eighteen runners to start at the extreme outside price of 200/1. Running the way the betting suggested, he finished unplaced to 'Buck' Barclay's great horse Bendigo.

Following his defeat in the Jubilee, Gallinule was off the course until turning out for the Great Yorkshire Handicap over a mile and three quarters at York's Ebor meeting in the middle of August. Evidently something better was expected of him as he was third favourite at 5/1 in an open market on a field of six with Lord Zetland's Panzerschiff favourite at 3/1. Even though beaten again, Gallinule managed to leave his spring form right behind by finishing second, beaten three parts of a length by Panzerschiff. Had not his misdeeds, or rather those that he committed at the behest of others, caught up with him within the hour, Billy Stomachache might have become hopeful that Gallinule was soon to fulfil the promise of his two-year-old days.

The race after the Great Yorkshire Handicap was the six-furlong Harewood Handicap, for which Tyler saddled the marquess's four-year-old Everitt. Two month's earlier, Everitt had won the Wokingham Stakes at Royal Ascot, and as he appeared to have a very good chance of supplementing this success, was joint favourite at 4/1. His running, however, left the nasty impression that it was not the money of connections that had made him that price.

After having jumped off smartly, Martin, Everitt's regular rider, seemed at no pains to keep his place until it became obvious that he had no option but to ride a finish. As a result of that late endeavour, Everitt was able to make a dead heat of it with Whittington. The bookmakers showed how certain they were that Everitt would have won outright had Martin begun to ride earlier by making him 6/1 on to win the deciding heat, which he did by three parts of a length.

At the subsequent inquiry, the stewards were unable to decide whether
Martin had ridden an ill-judged race by trying to win by too short a
distance or whether he had not tried to win at all. Accordingly, the case
was referred to the stewards of the Jockey Club.

The stewards of the Jockey Club, Lord Hastings, Mr H. W.
Fitzwilliam and Mr James Lowther, opened their inquiry at the
Doncaster St Leger meeting and concluded it at the Newmarket first
October meeting. Their verdict was a damning indictment of Ailesbury.
They pronounced themselves satisfied that he had, in the presence of
Tyler, told Martin not to win at York, where Martin was unable to carry
out those instructions only as a result of finding himself in front for too
long. The stewards were also satisfied that he had ordered horses to be
stopped on other occasions.

The 4th Marquess of Ailesbury was therefore warned off the Turf,
together with his trainer. In the case of Martin, the stewards tempered
justice with mercy by giving him a severe reprimand and cautioning him
as to his future conduct. The best that can be said for Billy Stomachache is
that his unedyfying exit from the Turf was more the price of
foolhardiness than villainy.

As a disqualified person, Billy Stomachache had no more use for his
horses than his abundance of creditors had long supposed to be the case.
Consequently they came up for sale later in the autumn, when the Squire,
as indifferent as ever to how he threw his money around, went up to 5,000
guineas for Gallinule. When the hammer fell, Billy Stomachache doffed
his hat and said to Mr Tattersall, 'Thank you, now I have some more
money for cards tonight.'

As Martin Gurry, then training for the Squire, ran his hands down
Gallinule's legs, somebody remarked, 'You have got a bargain there, Mr
Gurry.'

'I would rather have the money than the horse,' replied the cautious
Gurry, who was habitually suspicious of any purchase that the Squire
made off his own bat.

'But he is a nice colt,' insisted the man.

'It is a nice price, too,' snorted Gurry, who well knew the results that
the Squire would be expecting for that sort of outlay.

It was, indeed, a nice price, but Billy Stomachache had still better
reason for satisfaction. In view of what lay between them in the matter of
Dolly Tester's affections, he had not made it his business to warn the
Squire against buying a 'bleeder'.

Gallinule's addiction to breaking blood vessels must have soon become apparent, but it was not a problem with which Gurry had to live for long. When he and the Squire parted company early in the summer of 1888, Charlie Morton found Gallinule among the multitude of problems to which he was heir at Bedford Lodge. By the end of the season Gallinule had been unplaced in each of his seven races as a four-year-old, including the Jubilee, the Wokingham Stakes and the Cambridgeshire. Sammy Loates had been his regular rider, but the Squire himself had taken the mount on him in the Ovingdean Plate, a six-furlong handicap, at Brighton in August.

Early in the spring of 1889 there were growing hopes of Gallinule having got over his propensity to break blood vessels. Gurry therefore decided to get him ready for the Lincolnshire, for which he had a mere 7 stone 9 pounds, by reason of his consistent failure the previous year, and the Squire and his friends began backing him. Shortly before the race, Gallinule was an impressive winner of a trial in which he beat another Lincoln runner, Acme, by six lengths. Still more money piled on him after that, with the result that he started favourite at 7/1.

The form of the trial was more than good enough to win the Lincoln, but luck never was on the side of the Squire when he went for the gloves in a big way, any more than it was when he paid a long price for a horse, though Busybody had been an exception. Once under the pressure of racing again, Gallinule broke another blood vessel and finished unplaced to Sir Robert Jardine's Wise Man, who, in receipt of 13 pounds, beat Acme half a length. That made the winner 11 pounds inferior to Acme, whereas, on trial form, Gallinule was well in front of that horse.

After the heavy losses incurred over the Lincolnshire, it finally occurred to the Squire that he had struck a particularly bad bargain over Gallinule. Resolving to be out of the clownish-looking horse, he instructed Morton to accept any offer he could get.

In the summer Morton discovered that a young officer in the army, Captain Harry Greer, was interested in buying Gallinule, though he did not fancy paying as much as £1,000 and asked to be given until 10th July to make up his mind. Although his commission was in the Cameronians, Harry Greer was an Irishman who had been born at Moy, Co. Tyrone, the son of Lieutenant-General H. H. Greer. At the time when he entered into negotiations to buy Gallinule, he was thirty-four and looking for a stallion for his newly acquired Brownstown Stud on the outskirts of the Curragh.

Gallinule's appeal as a stallion lay in his being a big, strong masculine horse who had been good enough to win a race of the importance of the National Breeders Produce Stakes. Moreover, his pedigree held a particular attraction for Captain Greer, who had a partiality for both the offspring of Isonomy and members of the female family tracing to Cast Steel. That mare, who was the fifth dam of Gallinule, had been foaled sixty-one years previously in 1828. Why Captain Greer should have held her descendants in such esteem he never explained, and it is not at all easy to understand as they had shown no ability of any outstanding order, though Gamester won the St Leger in 1859 and Upas had made a dead heat of the French Derby in 1886.

Captain Greer was given his option on Gallinule until 10th July. On the day previous to that, the horse ran on Newmarket's July course and, instead of his value being enhanced the usual thing happened. He broke a small blood vessel and finished unplaced. Fearing that Greer might find out that had happened, Morton took the initiative the following morning by saying to him, 'Well, as I know Mr Baird wishes to sell, I will risk it and take £900.' In doing so, Morton knew, or thought he knew, that he was still asking a lot more than the value of the horse. The trouble was that Gallinule had become afflicted in the wind so that he bore the dual stigma of roarer and bleeder.

The price of £900 having been agreed upon subject to a veterinary examination, George Barrow, who was regarded as Newmarket's leading veterinary surgeon, went to Bedford Lodge to look at the horse. When he had ascertained that Gallinule was sound of limb, Barrow said, 'Now I would just like you to put a saddle and bridle on him to try his wind.'

Not wishing to be present when the moment of truth arrived, Morton made himself scarce with an excuse about having a runner in the first. 'I'll tell my head man,' he said. 'You'll have to excuse me now. I must get away.'

'Oh, I don't suppose it matters much, Mr Morton,' replied Barrow with almost unbelievable naïvety. 'I'm sure the horse is all right!' Little wonder that in his memoirs Charles Morton recalled the old ass as a 'kindly old man, one of the best in the world'.

All that the Squire could do on being told he was finally rid of Gallinule was to say he was 'sorry for the fellow who had bought him'.

Shortly afterwards Morton ran into Captain Greer, who said to him, 'Now, Mr Morton, you have been very kind over this matter and I want you to let me make you a little present. Would you give me the pleasure of accepting a cheque for £50.'

Willingly Morton gave him that pleasure. Later he did have the grace to feel a little shame at how the utter incompetence of George Barrow had facilitated the clinching of the deal with this generous and honourable man. As things fell out, though, it was Captain Greer who had the last laugh, and a very loud laugh it was.

Although none too fertile in his first few seasons at Brownstown, Gallinule eventually became one of the most successful and influential stallions of all time. The greatest of his offspring was, of course, Pretty Polly, winner of the One Thousand Guineas, Oaks and St Leger together with nineteen of her other twenty-one races, and ancestress in tail female line of Brigadier Gerard, the Derby winners St Paddy and Psidium as well as of a host of other important horses. Among the other sons and daughters of Gallinule were the 1907 Two Thousand Guineas winner Slieve Gallion, the St Leger winners Wildfowler (1898) and Night Hawk (1913) and the 1905 Cesarewitch winner Hammerkop, dam of the Derby winner Spion Kop. In all, Gallinule sired the winners of 663 races worth £316,963, headed the list of stallions in 1904 and 1905, was second twice and third twice.

It was nice of the Squire to be 'sorry for the fellow who bought him', but not really necessary.

13 THE FUTURE THROWS ITS SHADOW

BY the early weeks of 1890, clouds of foreboding were already gathering around the Squire. He was no longer the carefree young man he had been the previous year while riding winners at what was a quite unprecedented rate for an amateur.

The question of whether Martin Gurry was to be paid up for the full period of his contract was still unresolved and legal action beginning to look increasingly imminent. Still worse, the Squire was more than ever under the influence of the prize-fighting fraternity, particularly the avaricious Charlie Mitchell who could always be relied upon to profit more than almost anybody else from the open-handedness of his patron. Whenever the Squire ran out of ideas for how to pass the time of day in a congenially moronic manner, Mitchell would rectify the deficiency in the agenda.

The first of the shadows over the Squire was cast by the intimation that the stewards of the Jockey Club were only prepared to grant him provisional permission to ride against professional jockeys until the lawsuit over the settlement of Gurry's contract had been heard. Jealous of the good name that racing had only recently acquired, they were more than a little apprehensive of the effect of washing any dirty linen belonging to the Squire in open court. The Turf's new-found respectability had been more than a little shaken by the warning off of the champion jockey, Charlie Wood, and the ensuing spate of rumours about fixing by a jockeys' ring, two years previously. If the way of life of the most successful Gentleman Rider of all times was to be made public knowledge by deft cross-examination, racing would inevitably take another step back into the mire from which Admiral Rous had begun to drag it in the middle of the century.

For once the Squire obliged the Jockey Club, though entirely for his own convenience. Rather than have them withdraw that temporary permission they had given so grudgingly, he settled with Martin Gurry out of court. In view of the extensive use Gurry was to make of the money he received, it would seem he had a bit more than the pound of flesh that was his due. In all probability he made the Squire pay for the aggravation he had been caused as well as for the balance of the time of his contract.

So great had been the Jockey Club's fear and abhorrence of the Squire that one of its leading members, the Earl of Durham, asked his brother George Lambton not to accept the ride on Bellona in the Grand National of 1890. Bellona was one of the best steeplechasers the Squire ever owned. She had finished fourth in the Grand National of 1889, and would have won the Grand Steeplechase de Paris had she not been brought down by a loose horse at the last fence.

With George Lambton complying with his brother's request, Harry Barker came in for the ride, but Bellona, who was second favourite at 11/2, unseated him at Becher's, and, carrying on riderless, staked herself horribly. So serious was her injury that it was only with great difficulty that they got her back to Newmarket, where, despite the pain she was in, she whinnied with pleasure at being home as she hobbled into her box at Bedford Lodge. Even then the battle for her life was lost and a few days later she died.

Harry Barker, who was both a good and a versatile jockey, never did win the Grand National. Three years after riding Bellona, he had the heart-breaking experience of being second in the Grand National on Aesop and then second in the Derby on Ravensbury.

Not only was the Squire in deeper disfavour than usual with the Jockey Club in the spring of 1890, and in ever more intimate association with dubious characters, but he was beginning to lose his enthusiasm for race riding, so recently the ruling passion of his life. Although still only twenty-eight years of age, he was feeling the effects of indulgence in constant, reckless revelry at the same time as wasting hard to keep down to a racing weight. The candle had been burning at both ends for too long. Soon the damage would be beyond repair of the longest purse, and his, despite his determination to spend, was still a long one.

The Rejected, one of the favourite mounts of the Squire, who won thirteen races on him. According to a tradition in the family of Mr Tony Sweeney, the owner of the painting, the rider is in fact the Squire

LEFT: *Lillie Langtry, as beautiful as she was acquisitive* BBC HULTON PICTURE LIBRARY

RIGHT: *Charlie Mitchell, Champion of England and mug punter, the Squire's philosopher, guide and friend* MARY EVANS PICTURE LIBRARY

BELOW LEFT: *Jem Smith, whom the Squire backed so heavily in what turned out to be the 'affair at Bruges' (pp 122–124)* MARY EVANS PICTURE LIBRARY

BELOW RIGHT: *Jem Mace, 'The Swaffham Gypsy', helped to restore the good name of boxing by his sportmanship but in middle age allowed himself to fawn on the Squire* MARY EVANS PICTURE LIBRARY

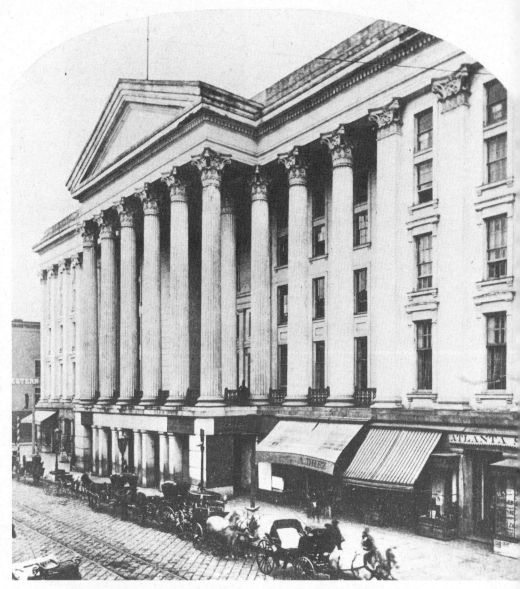

The St Charles Hotel, New Orleans, in which the Squire died of a fever on 18 March 1893 MANSELL COLLECTION

For those that wanted to read it, the writing was on the wall when the Squire failed to ride at the opening meeting of the season at Lincoln, where each of the four runners from Bedford Lodge was placed. These included the two-year-old Macuncas, on whom Tom Cannon was second in the Brocklesby Stakes. By then a veteran of forty-four, Tom Cannon, knowing the capriciousness of the Squire, and mindful, perhaps, that age could devalue his services, declined the renewal of his retainer of £3,000 a year. Instead he demanded, and received, a retainer for three years at that rate, the £9,000 to be paid in a lump sum in advance. Allowing for the devaluation of money, it was a bargain which his great-grandson Lester Piggott might be proud to strike.

At Liverpool, where the Squire had his first mount of the season on the unplaced Lyddington, things went better than at Lincoln. Macuncas won the Molyneux Stakes and Father Confessor the Liverpool Spring Cup. For what would not be the only time that year, Tom Cannon was unable to do the weight for Father Confessor, on whom Sammy Loates deputized.

In buying Father Confessor, a well-named son of The Abbot and Still-Room, for the Squire at the December sales of the previous year, Charlie Morton had taken a big risk. The four-year-old was a cast-off from old Tom Jennings's Lagrange stable, and everybody knew his horses worked harder than anything else on Newmarket Heath so that once he had finished with one there was not much horse left. Father Confessor, a mean wiry brown who looked as though he had been off his feed for weeks, gave every indication of having been right through the Jennings routine.

On approaching Jennings before the sale, Morton learned that the horse was perfectly sound in wind and limb but a martyr to cracked heels. After Edmund Tattersall's hammer had fallen at 900 guineas, Jennings vouchsafed the more categorical information that Father Confessor would never win a race.

Charlie Morton was not despondent. Some of those age-old country methods he had learned from rough-and-ready Tom Parr twenty years previously could still be more effective than those of the veterinary surgeons, and he had always had a way with cracked heels, a kind of eczema resulting from the oils being washed out of the skin. Before long the heels responded to treatment, and above them Father Confessor put on weight and condition so that he looked more like a well-fed friar than a mendicant monk. Tom Jennings, who saw him being galloped, could not help noticing the improvement and had the effrontery to ask if he should have his fiver on at Liverpool, where his former charge duly won the cup without being out of a canter.

Having paid such scant regard to those first meetings of the season, the Squire began to take his riding seriously again for a while. On Easter Monday he won on his old favourite The Rejected, still fresh from a great triumph in the Lincolnshire, at Kempton Park. Three days later he was successful on Laceman, running in the name of Tom Stevens, at Northampton, and soon afterwards won the High Peak Handicap at another now-defunct meeting, Derby, where he brought Freemason home a comfortable four lengths clear of Warlaby. The runner-up was ridden by the great northern jockey, Johnny Osborne, who had his first mount in public fifteen years before the Squire was born.

Meanwhile the rejuvenated Father Confessor continued to go from strength to strength and was strongly fancied for the Great Cheshire Handicap at Chester in early May. On the first day of the Chester meeting, 'Rosebery' Smith reappeared at Morton's side, rather like a fairy whose offer to grant a wish had already been rejected once.

'A couple of years ago,' he said, 'when you were a little younger than you are now, I offered you a horse and you would not have him. Now, although I do not know why I should give you the chance, I want to tell you that I have another just as good. The price is the same as before, £4,000, will you have this one?' Then he went on to declare that the horse, whose name was Tyrant, would win the Chester Cup, and however much Father Confessor might be fancied, the Great Cheshire handicap on the following day too.

As 'Rosebery' Smith was going no better than he had been when he had tried to sell Goldseeker two years previously, Morton suspected that the old man was trying to play on memories of the self-recrimination that followed the refusal of that horse and asking the identical price just to aggravate them. Therefore, on the principal that lightning never strikes twice in the same place, and in consideration of the price being a distinctly steep one, the offer was refused.

Just as Goldseeker had been at Doncaster, Tyrant was as good as 'Rosebery' Smith's word. On the Wednesday he justified favouritism with Seth Chandley up in the Chester Cup, and then, on the Thursday, defied a 14-pound penalty by beating Father Confessor a length. For good measure, Tyrant then proceeded to win the Gold Vase (now the Queen's Vase), the Doncaster Cup and two of his four other races during the remainder of the season.

In view of the huge sums that the Squire paid for some really bad horses, it is one of the minor ironies of racing that he opted for misplaced prudence in the cases of both Goldseeker and Tyrant.

Possibly the Squire's disinclination to give £4,000 for Tyrant was due to his still feeling more than a little foolish over having paid a lot of money for a very poor animal called Quartus the previous winter. For that indifferent specimen of thoroughbred flesh, he gave Harry Hall, who trained at Spigot Lodge, Middleham, the almost unheard-of sum of £6,000, a price greatly in excess of the then record for a yearling.

The form of Quartus was well to the leeward of the reputation that inspired the Squire to pay so much for him, his only success in two seasons having been obtained under 6 stone 7 pounds in a nursery at Manchester. All the same, the Squire suddenly said to Morton one day in a manner he fondly thought suggested he knew more than he was telling, 'Old Harry Hall has a horse called Quartus which he wants me to buy.'

'What's he asking for him?' inquired Morton apprehensively.

'Six thousand pounds.'

'That's a lot of money,' said Morton.

'Yes,' said the Squire, as though he were about to do something exceedingly clever. 'But what does it matter if it is for a good horse?'

Quartus, then a four-year-old, duly arrived at Bedford Lodge, where he was seen to be a fine big chestnut who moved impressively in his slow paces. Charlie Morton gave him the engagements in the City and Suburban and the other good handicaps, and as soon as he was fit tried him with the classic horse Pioneer, Father Confessor, Lady Rosebery and Snaplock on the Limekilns. Tommy Loates rode Quartus, and Tom Cannon, Sammy Loates, Jack Watts and another of the top jockeys the others. With tackle like that to take him along, Quartus was being tried high, even for an expensive horse, but he answered the question in no uncertain manner by finishing stone-cold motherless last.

Morton was astounded, the Squire furious. To give vent to his displeasure, the Squire rushed off to tell Harry Hall exactly what he thought of him. Harry Hall reacted with pained surprise, or pretended to, and without offering to have the horse back went round to Bedford Lodge to find out what had happened.

'I can't understand it,' he moaned to Charlie Morton. 'I never trained a better horse.'

'Well, I never trained a worse one,' observed Morton dryly.

Even if Harry Hall was telling the truth, it was not unduly high praise of Quartus. For the most part the Middleham trained confined his attention to selling platers and moderate handicappers though he had won the Northumberland Plate with Harriet Laws in 1875.

Although the likelihood of Quartus winning was too remote for contemplation, there had been nothing else to do but let him take his chance in the City and Suburban. With friends such as the Squire had, there was no question of his also having stable secrets, so all Newmarket knew what had happened in the trial on the Limekilns and Quartus was allowed to start at 40/1 at Epsom, where he finished unplaced to the 1887 Oaks winner Rêve d'Or, ridden by Tom Cannon's sixteen-year-old son Morny. Quartus showed no more inclination to race when down the field on both his other appearances that season, but the Squire, stubborn as ever, kept his inordinately expensive purchase in training, determined that he would come good one day.

The next engagement fulfilled by Father Confessor after Chester was the £2,000 Manchester Cup at the Whitsun meeting on the New Barns course. Also in the field was the previous season's Oaks winner, L'Abbesse de Jouarre, known to the bookmakers as 'Abscess on the Jaw'. She was trained by Bob Sherwood for Lord Randolph Churchill, the father of Sir Winston Churchill.

Rather than put up overweight on Father Confessor, as Charlie Morton wanted him to do, Tom Cannon begged off riding the Squire's horse and went off to have some lunch, a luxury a jockey close to the end of his career can afford, while Morton followed, pleading with him to change his mind. At the dining room door they met Lord Randolph Churchill, who asked Cannon to ride L'Abbesse de Jouarre.

'I'm afraid I can't, my lord,' said Cannon. 'I have missed riding one of our own and I should hardly like to get up on anything else. Also I am certain that I cannot do the weight.'

'That doesn't matter,' replied Lord Randolph. 'I'll have you, even if you have to put up a pound or two over. Come along Tom, I would be ever so much obliged to you if you would.'

Cannon gave Morton a sideways look as he said, 'But I have just told Mr Morton that I cannot ride Father Confessor and I really don't like riding yours.'

But Lord Randolph, one of the most compelling speakers in the House of Commons, was not to be denied and, wheedling away, succeeded where Morton had failed, in persuading Tom Cannon to ride at overweight.

Most onlookers agreed Tom Cannon would have won the Manchester Cup on either. Superior jockeyship decided the issue, and L'Abbesse de Jouarre, ridden by Cannon at 8 stone 8 pounds, gave Father Confessor, Sammy Loates up, 3 pounds and a beating of three parts of a length.

Mindful of the £9,000 that he paid for first call on Cannon's services, the Squire was livid.

'How was it,' he asked Morton, 'that Cannon did not ride Father Confessor?'

'He could not do the weight,' replied Morton. 'He rode the mare overweight.'

'It would not have mattered if he had ridden Father Confessor three or four pounds overweight,' said the Squire angrily. 'Anyway, I don't think it right,' he added in that peevish way of his, 'and I feel very dissatisfied and annoyed.'

'Well,' said Morton a bit sheepishly, 'I'm afraid I must take the blame. I was present when Lord Randolph put the matter to him.'

'All right,' reported the Squire. 'Now you go to him and tell him what I say.' Morton crossed over to Cannon, and, keeping his back to their employer, who was watching them, said, 'Don't take a bit of notice of what I am going to say, Tom. He says you are everything that is rotten. If you had your dues you would be shot at dawn and he hopes you will never ride another winner as long as you live.'

Relieved at the mildness of the rebuke, Tom burst out laughing and said, 'I dare say he does feel a bit cross. Tell him it won't happen again.'

'What did he say?' asked the Squire when Morton returned. 'Did he apologize?'

'Yes, he did, and he says it will never happen again.'

'That's all right then,' said the Squire, suddenly mollified.

Not for the first time he had found himself paying out money for less than nothing. Having retained the best jockey in the country, he had to watch that jockey riding another man's horse to beat his own runner in one of the biggest races of the season. Yet he bore no malice. Quite one of the most attractive characteristics of the Squire was his complete inability to harbour a grudge.

Sammy Loates, who rode Father Confessor in the Manchester Cup, was an ugly, aggressive little man with bushy eyebrows, heavily hooded eyes and a bulbous nose, while, like his brothers, Ben and Tommy, he had unusually short legs, even for a jockey. Sammy was one of the Squire's favourite riders, and it was not only his equestrian talent that recommended him to his patron. Always addicted to rough riding, and occasionally foul, he had a breadth of vocabulary and felicitous command of vivid language that held the Squire spellbound. Back in the days of his apprenticeship, he had made himself so conspicuous for his coarseness, even by the standards prevalent in a stable dormitory, that he had been dubbed 'Burglar Bill' in allusion to Dickens's foul-mouthed Bill Sykes.

Sammy was not everybody's jockey. True, the fastidious Lord Rosebery employed him, but Harding Cox, who rode against him, was moved to write, 'I knew the Loates bunch. Ben often sported my "two greens", and I think Tommy did on one occasion – Sam never!'

In the matter of Father Confessor and L'Abbesse de Jouarre, the Squire, for once, had his compensation. The two horses met again in the Liverpool Summer Cup in July when Father Confessor was reunited with Tom Cannon and beat Lord Randolph Churchill's filly, Jack Watts up, by a length.

The race after the Liverpool Cup was the seven-furlong County Welter Selling Handicap, in which horses ridden by professional jockeys had to carry 6-pound penalties. The Squire rode Mirabeau for Mr Blundell Maple, whose fortune came from his furniture emporium in London's Tottenham Court Road, while the favourite, Orange Peel, owned and trained by Tom Cannon's brother Joe, carried the extra weight for the services of Fred Webb.

These two horses had the finish to themselves, but by the time they reached the post not all the strength and driving of Webb could shake off the Squire. The judge called a dead heat, and as connections could not agree to divide the stakes, a deciding heat had to be run. The outcome of that was all but the same as it had been in the original race, with the professionally ridden Orange Peel prevailing by no more than a short head. To have enabled a horse to reproduce its form to the fraction of an ounce against one ridden by a jockey of the calibre of Fred Webb was a remarkable achievement on the part of the Squire and showed what a great race rider he was when fit and sober. Fred Webb had won the Derby of 1873 on Doncaster at the age of twenty, and, in a golden age of British jockeyship dominated by Archer, Fordham and Cannon, he had few superiors.

To have forced a dead heat with Webb and to have nearly beaten him in the run-off would have delighted the Squire infinitely more than owning any number of big race winners. The feeling of exhilaration left by that great performance strengthened his resolve to resume riding with the same regularity that he had done the previous year.

But he was now nearly thirty, and, ominously, what had been a tall, spare frame in early manhood was beginning to put on flesh. Only by severe dieting, that must have been excruciatingly painful, and a great deal of exercise, could he maintain a racing weight.

One Wednesday evening in the August of 1890, he had just three or four ounces of sweetbreads and a large dose of medicine for his dinner. The following morning he tramped eight miles in heavy sweaters before returning to a breakfast of two ounces of fish. After that he allowed himself no more food until half past nine in the evening, when he had another four ounces of sweetbread and more medicine, probably something akin to 'Archer's Mixture', the powerful purgative with which the great Fred had kept body and soul together. In between those two spartan repasts, the millionaire would have walked a dozen miles to the Turkish baths and ridden two or three races. The expenditure of energy was so hopelessly out of proportion to the intake of nutriment that his constitution inevitably had to suffer.

By adherence to that drastic régime, the Squire was able to get down to 9 stone 12 pounds, to win on Maley a race for horses ridden by Members of the Club at Lewes on 9th August when he was completing a treble after having been successful on Tom Wadlow's Westminster and Devil's Own earlier in the afternoon. Devil's Own ran in the name of George Masterman, one of his numerous secretaries. Ned Baird also had a winner at that Lewes meeting when Flodden Field, ridden by Tom Cannon, beat The Deemster in the Astley Stakes.

The following week the Squire could not even do 10 stone and had to put up a pound overweight at 10 stone 1 pound to win on White Wings at Windsor, where he was also successful on Charleston the same afternoon. Both horses were entered as the property of his Chilton trainer, William Stevens.

As a result of still more rigorous wasting, he got down to 9 stone 12 pounds again to win on Secretaire at Lichfield later in the month, during which he also won races on both that course and Wolverhampton on Bob Armstrong's Ashton, and another even at Wolverhampton on The Mummer. Thus nine winners which he rode during a period of intense activity and virtual starvation that August brought his tally for the season to twenty-five.

After the lassitude of early spring, which ruined his chance of equalling, let alone surpassing, his great record of 1889, he was riding as well as ever again despite the privation entailed in severe wasting. Meanwhile Charlie Mitchell and the other unwholesome bullies he had picked up were just waiting for the time when he would finish riding, which had almost become his lifeline to sanity, so that they could take control of him and his fortune.

As usual the autumn found him back in Scotland for the Western meeting at Ayr. From two mounts on the first day he won on The Solent for Bob Armstrong and was placed on the other, was placed again on both the horses that he rode on the second day, and made three more mounts on the third day into a treble by winning on Mr G. MacLachlan's Turkish Delight and Mr R. Weighell's Linthorpe, and then on Sly Fellow, owned by the Newmarket trainer, Tom Leader, father of the late Harvey Leader and grandfather of Ted Leader. The following month the Squire was in the same sort of form at the two-day meeting at Worcester, where he rode four winners and walked over on another. Among his successful mounts at that fixture was Brucea, owned by the veteran East Ilsey, Berkshire, trainer, Jim Dover, who had turned out Lord Lyon to win the Triple Crown back in 1866. By giving the Squire the ride on Brucea in the City Welter Handicap, Dover was able to take advantage of the 5-pound allowance to which Gentleman Riders were entitled by the conditions of the race.

Early in November the Squire's mare, Lady Rosebery, returned to Aintree to win the Liverpool Autumn Cup. In a ding-dong battle between two of the Loates brothers, Sammy on the mare beat Tommy on Shall We Remember by a neck, with Father Confessor, Tom Cannon up again, unplaced. Six days later the Squire rode his forty-second and final winner of the season by getting Jack Hammond's Cigar Light home by three parts of a length from Ashton with his old adversary Fred Webb in the saddle.

Although he had ridden barely two thirds as many winners as he had done the previous season, the Squire was still the undisputed champion of the Gentlemen Riders. A very remote second, with five winners to his credit, was thirty-year-old George Lambton, who would take over the Bedford Lodge stable as private trainer to Lord Derby in three years' time. Third in the list was Willie Moore, the large genial Irishman, with four winners; then came the Sussex baronet, Sir James Duke, with three, and Arthur Coventry and Mr J. Craig with two apiece. Among those who rode just one winner in 1890 were Ned Baird, who had been successful on Tom Cannon's Duke of Richmond at the Bibury Club meeting, 'Buck' Barclay, Ronnie Moncreiffe and Henry Milner.

14 THE SQUIRE AND THE LILY

THOSE of an uncharitable disposition used to say that Lillie Langtry was purpose-bred on her sire's side. Certain it is that the good people of Jersey remembered her father as 'The Dirty Dean', long after he had departed from their midst, leaving many of the younger islanders bearing a most remarkable likeness to himself. Indeed, the venerable gentleman was obliged to bring the very first of all Lillie's romances to an abrupt conclusion on account of her juvenile fancy being her half-brother.

Emilie Charlotte Le Breton, whom the world knows as Lillie Langtry, was born in Jersey on 13th October 1853, the daughter of the Ven. William Corbet Le Breton, Dean of Jersey and Rector of St Saviours, and his wife, formerly Miss Emilie Martin of King's Parade, Chelsea. By the time she reached womanhood, Lillie was hard to fault, a rare beauty by the standards of any age. Her eyes were a mixture of blue and purple, sparkling like clusters of amethysts and sapphires in bright sunlight, her hair Titian fair, her skin a flawless white and her features cast in the classical Greek mould. In addition she had a full but graceful figure and the poise to carry it superbly.

From the age of fifteen she had a steady stream of suitors, including the son of an Archbishop of Canterbury. Although no more were rendered unacceptable by consanguinity, Lillie found them all too poor or too dull and often both. Eventually, to obtain the independence of her parents that she wanted so badly, she accepted the proposal of the widower Edward Langtry, who at least passed muster on one score. They were married on 9th March 1874.

Edward Langtry, whose first wife had died two years previously within three years of marriage, was the grandson of Richard Langtry, founder of the shipping line that plied the lucrative route between his native Belfast and Liverpool. By contrast to his enterprising grandfather, Edward Langtry was an unintelligent, listless individual. Unable to play any useful part in the running of the family firm, he settled down to a futile existence in Jersey, spending most of his time on board his beautiful yacht, *Red Gauntlet*, which carried a crew of five. In later years, when her fondness for luxury yachts had become still more pronounced, Lillie used to admit that she had only married the wretched man for *Red Gauntlet*.

Once unshackled from parental control, Lillie was impatient to be away from her tiny homeland, to see the world and make her impact on it. To gratify that desire, Edward Langtry took her to live in London and thereafter receded into an alcoholic background with the same rapidity as she became established as what was called a 'PB' in upper-class jargon. Professional beauties were young ladies whose marriages gave them status rather than commitment, leaving them free to confer the ultimate favour where they pleased. The ultimate favour was generally conferred when gentlemen called for afternoon tea, but 'PB's' were also acceptable guests at receptions and dinner parties as well as country-house parties, where the ultimate favour could be conferred very easily indeed.

While in London, Lillie was to be seen riding in Rotten Row or driving in the park with a wide variety of escorts. So high were the passions that she could arouse that Londoners were once treated to the unedifying sight of a public brawl between a former senior steward of the Jockey Club and a future holder of that august office. She had been riding in Rotten Row with Lord Lonsdale when she stopped to speak to Sir George Chetwynd, who was on foot. Sir George complained that she should have been riding with him, whereupon Lord Lonsdale jumped from the saddle and knocked him down. Further fisticuffs ensued until the Duke of Portland and Sir William Gordon-Cumming intervened to separate the gallants.

The first meeting between Lillie and the Prince of Wales took place at a supper party given by the Arctic explorer, Sir Allen Young, at his house in Stratford Place, London, on 27th May 1877. The prince saw that reports that he had received of her from Lord Hartington and other members of the Marlborough House set had not been exaggerated by the slightest bit, and within days she was his acknowledged mistress.

Another of Lillie's exalted lovers in the early 1880s was Prince Louis of

Battenburg, an officer in the Royal Navy, who later married the Prince of Wales's niece, Princess Alice of Hesse. The torrid affair between Prince Louis and Lillie came to an end when he was ordered to sea aboard the warship bearing the appropriate name of *Inconstant*. A few months later, Lillie retired discreetly to Paris to give birth to his daughter, who was christened Jeanne-Marie, on 8th March 1881.

The only disadvantage that Lillie suffered through estrangement from her husband was an acute shortage of money. To rectify the situation, she took to acting, for which she had shown aptitude in amateur dramatics, and made her professional début in a comedy called *Ours* at the Haymarket Theatre early in 1882. The Prince of Wales gave her all the encouragement and support that he could, making the journey from Sandringham to see her performance towards the end of January, again the following month, and once more in March.

Although the Prince of Wales was loyal to his friends, he was hardly faithful in love. After nearly ten years of liaison with Lillie, he found fresh distractions, and Lillie, throwing all her energy into her theatrical career, went on tour in the United States, from which country she returned in 1888.

Among the expensive undertakings to which Lillie aspired was the ownership of racehorses. She was an inveterate racegoer, a taste that she probably acquired from the Prince of Wales, and it was at Newmarket that she met George Baird on 28th April 1891.

She was about to place a bet on the first race, and the Squire, overhearing her, insisted that she should change her mind and back his runner, even though it was the unpredictable Quartus that carried his colours. In cold and measured terms that should have done nothing to encourage further solicitude for her punting, she let him know that she picked her own fancies, but the Squire, well aware that the way to her bed was through her purse rather than her heart, undertook to reimburse her to the tune of three times her stake if his horse were beaten. Then, for good measure, he gave her a roll of notes with which to back his three-year-old Macuncas for herself later in the afternoon.

Quartus, with uncharacteristic cooperation, duly justified the Squire's confidence by winning at 5/2, and then in the third race, for which he was 7/4 on, Macuncas beat Vivarium, owned, trained and ridden by Tom Cannon. That evening Lillie accepted an invitation to dine with her new benefactor.

Despite the fact that she was playing to full houses all the time, Lillie was not without her difficulties. Maintaining her house in Pont Street, dressing in the manner expected of a leading actress and still prominent member of London society, and covering the many other expenses that a husband would normally pay, confronted her with frequent problems. In the circumstances, the friendship of a millionaire would have been most acceptable had the millionaire been a bit more so.

As she was a fastidious woman of undoubted charm and wit, Lillie should have been repelled by everything about the Squire. With his devotion to riding, boxing, cards, cock-fighting and continuous drinking, he was very much a man's man. Yet, before she came to know his terrifying temper, she seemed to find something attractive in him. It was as though their sharply contrasting qualities produced a chemical reaction resulting in the exquisitely refined woman of the world being drawn by the almost animal magnetism of the vigorously virile man, eight years her junior. Where she should have been disgusted she seemed fascinated. Nevertheless she had no qualms about becoming what the Squire's detractors regarded as little more than a mobster's moll, even on occasion going as far as letting herself be fondled in public.

Throughout May 1891, the Squire was a regular caller at the Pont Street house. He and Lillie were often to be seen together dining *à deux* in the West End after the theatre, or in each other's company at Sandown Park, Kempton or one of the other metropolitan meetings before she returned to town for the evening show. Never hitherto discriminating in his taste for women, or anything else but horses, the Squire was every bit as besotted by her loveliness, which she preserved so well as middle age approached, as her rather more selective lovers before him. He was as proud of being her escort as he was of his riding, and dreamed of the day when he could marry her.

The money he had spent on Dolly Tester and his other women looked almost paltry in comparison with what he lavished on Lillie. Day after day presents that he had ordered from the most expensive jewellers in London would be delivered to Pont Street. He even gave her two of his precious thoroughbreds, yearlings that he had bred at the Kentford stud. One of them was the colt by Saraband out of Colleen Bawn II who was to be given the name of Milford. Even Lillie, who had dined with princes and had been a guest at the most exclusive house-parties in England, was staggered by his extravagance. When dining in a hotel or restaurant, they would be surrounded by discarded champagne bottles still three quarters full because, he said, only the wine from the top of the bottle was worth drinking.

For all his generosity, the Squire had his drawbacks as a lover. The most serious of these was obsessive jealousy. No nun could have been more closely cloistered than Lillie would have been in Pont Street had he had his way. He flew into the most fearful rages if he found her receiving another man in the house.

As soon as the object of his resentment had taken leave of Lillie rather than endure his surly rudeness, the Squire would give vent to his feelings in a very much more forcible manner by belabouring her with his fists, and the drunker he was the longer and harder he pummelled her. More than one of her women friends, finding her nursing a black eye, asked her why she submitted to such treatment. Quite candidly she admitted that she did not love him, but went on to explain, quite practicably, that every time he beat her up he gave her a cheque for £5,000.

A much less dramatic result of giving herself to the Squire, though nevertheless a painful one, afforded her no such consolation. Whereas society hostesses had once besieged her with invitations, knowing her presence to be essential if there were to be any chance of the Prince of Wales attending their functions, the great ladies of the land now almost all ignored her. Nobody wanted the 'Jersey Lily' escorted by a man they considered no more than a drunken jockey, without even the good manners of the professionals like Cannon and Watts. As for the Squire, he was more unpopular than ever with the male members of the Establishment. Too many had failed ignominiously where he had succeeded so completely for them to like him any better.

In the autumn of 1891, the Squire returned to Scotland, as he usually did at that season of the year. This time, though, it was not to ride at the Western meeting at Ayr, where he only had one runner, but to follow Lillie round on her tour of provincial theatres in the northern kingdom. Although not averse to playing the angel by backing her productions financially, he never carried his admiration of her to the length of watching a complete performance. While Lillie acted, he drank in a near-by bar until it was time to go to the stage door to take her to dinner.

There was, however, just one occasion on which the Squire allowed himself an active interest in the theatre. Lillie was resting in Pont Street one Sunday afternoon when she received an urgent summons to the Haymarket. On arrival she found pandemonium in the foyer, where the barking of dogs was accompanied by the high-pitched squeals of smaller animals while the Squire and his friends were shouting above each others' voices as they offered abuse and encouragement according to the interests of their pockets. To pass the sabbath afternoon, the Squire had matched his dog against that of one of his cronies in a rat-catching contest, the foyer of Lily's theatre having been agreed upon as the arena. Thirty-two of the vermin were let loose from a sack, in accordance with the rules, and the dog that killed the most acclaimed the winner. Nauseated by the sight of so much blood-letting and the sound of crunching bones, Lillie fled without waiting for the result.

At the end of Lillie's Scottish tour, she returned to London while he remained for a few days' shooting on the moors. By this time she was beginning to have serious misgivings about their relationship, notwithstanding its enormous pecuniary advantages.

A few days after her return to town, Lillie was walking down Oxford Street when she met Robert Peel, a lanky, rather uninteresting young man of ample means, who was always at pains to press his company on her. On Peel suggesting that he should take her to Paris for a few days, she accepted the offer, purely as a gesture of her independence of the Squire rather than from any desire to listen to endless protestations of Bobby Peel's devotion to her. The tedium of his company, she would make sure, was alleviated by his buying her the new gowns that she badly needed from the exclusive salon of Monsieur Worth in the Rue de la Paix.

When the Squire got back to London to find that she had gone to Paris with another man, he flew into a towering rage and set off after them to deal with the matter in his own inimitable way. Arriving in Paris in a drunken, vicious fury, he went straight to their hotel and burst into the private suite in which they were sitting. Hard and fit from his riding, he made short work of the inoffensive, foppish Bobby Peel, while Lillie looked on with the horrific certainty of what was to follow. Having knocked the man, for whom he had worked up a blind hatred, all over the luxuriously appointed room, regardless of the damage done in the process, the Squire kicked him out on to the landing, impatient to wreak his vengeance on the principal object of his displeasure. In that alcoholic frenzy of jealous rage, he then gave her the worst beating she had ever had from him, and when the proximity of her body aroused his sexual appetite, he tore away her clothes to sink his teeth into her skin and claw at it with his nails in a terrible intensity of animal passion. Even when the 'Jersey Lily' was a whimpering mass of blood and bruises, the Squire was still not satisfied with his revenge, to which he put the finishing touches by smashing to pieces everything that had survived his earlier activity and ripping the contents of her wardrobe to shreds. Then he left as the hotel maids came to the room in reply to her screams for help.

As a result of the dreadful injuries the Squire had done her, Lillie was in hospital for a fortnight, nursing two black eyes, a swollen nose and various other uncomfortable disfigurements under swathes of bandages. Rumours that she had been disfigured for life by the demonic Gentleman Rider swept Paris and London, but to the intense disappointment of certain members of her own sex, these eventually proved unfounded.

A warrant for the arrest of the Squire was issued as soon as Lillie was well enough to talk to the *gendarmes*. As it happened, he was already in their custody, heavily hung over, following the disturbance he had caused in the brothel to which he had repaired after the fracas at the hotel.

Upon the issue of the warrant, the Squire was taken to the hospital under escort so that Lillie could make a formal identification of him before he was charged. But, to the utter amazement of the *gendarmerie*, his victim withdrew her complaint almost as soon as he began to plead for her forgiveness, grovelling at the bedside, and as he soon afterwards made restitution to the hotel on a scale suggesting to the management that Monsieur Baird was a gentleman after all, he had to be released.

The whole charade must have convinced the *gendarmes* that the British are mad. Had they known, though, it was with all the clarity of Gallic logic that Lily reasoned there was a great deal more to be had in atonement from a badly frightened and chastened Squire outside a French gaol than there would be from an embittered Squire inside a French gaol.

In this she was absolutely right, but even her acquisitive optimism could not have foreseen how he was to give thanks for delivery from the most unpleasant retribution he had ever faced or deserved. In addition to a cheque for £50,000, ten times the standard fee, he gave her a three-masted schooner-rigged yacht that he bought from the impoverished Lord Ashburton for £20,000. Lily called called her yacht the *Whyte Lady*. To everybody else the vessel of atonement was known as the 'Black Eye'.

15 LORD OF THE RING

THAT the Squire should have become a patron of the prize ring was in the natural order of things. As a member of the leisured classes, he had so much time on his hands that it was quite impossible for him to devote anything like all of it to racing, especially as he had such a strong distaste for going to a meeting without the certainty of a mount.

Everything about boxing was calculated to make it the sport of his second, and in due course his first, allegiance. Not only was it time-honoured as a manly pursuit, but it had a vigorous flamboyance all of its own, and its devotees formed an exclusive coterie, to which he was pleased to find himself a great deal more acceptable than he was to the Jockey Club. Most important of all, perhaps, he liked the earthy characters of the prize-fighters and their vividly forceful jargon that he used so well himself.

His entry into the world of prize-fighting was, of course, as fortuitous as that of Alice into Wonderland. A passion for race riding had brought him to Newmarket, but it was there that he had met up with Charlie Mitchell and the other followers of the fighting game who patronized the Greyhound in Bill Riley's time as landlord of that hostelry. There he had acquired his enthusiasm for pugilism, and although the fighting men could never redeem their promise to teach him enough of their art to make a champion of him, their constant companionship henceforward was a guarantee that his ambition to be a patron of champions would never be abated.

Unlike racing, however, prize-fighting was still a long way from having recovered from the depths of disrepute into which it had been dragged by venal pugs and the sleazy, greedy gamblers who controlled them in the middle years of the century. Indeed, prize-fighting was so far from rehabilitation as to be still illegal, though an increasing number of influential men were rallying to its cause.

As far back as 1867, the use of gloves had become mandatory with the introduction of the Queensberry Rules, which were drawn up to give the Noble Art a respectability that it had lacked so long. By the time the Squire arrived upon the scene, Lord Lonsdale, Sir John Astley and others were carrying on the struggle to regain the good name of prize-fighting. They all belonged to the Pelican Club, of which the Squire was an extremely prominent member by reason of his sponsorship of a whole stable of fighters.

The Pelican Club had started life as the Star Club in premises at 21 Denman Street, a thoroughfare at the southern end of Shaftesbury Avenue, and was opened on Wednesday, 19th January 1887, a few weeks before Merry Hampton won the Derby. Its object was to provide a rendezvous for supper and nocturnal recreation for young men about town of sporting inclinations. The said young men had previously taken their ease at the Adelphi Club in Covent Garden until management and staff had become increasingly supercilious, disdainful of cashing cheques for small amounts, and reluctant to provide early-morning tripe-and-onion suppers after the hotels, restaurants and chop houses had closed for the night in conformity with the highly unpopular new Licensing Act.

In consequence of the cool and inimical attitude encountered there, the secessionist members created a much more congenial atmosphere at the Star, where there was a boxing saloon, a champagne bar, a cocktail bar (that fashionable innovation from the United States), a supper room and other amenities to cater for the needs of the fancy. Unfortunately, the backer for the new club, a Lewisham grocer, was so convinced by its immediate success that he had found the formula for wealth untold that he became apt to celebrate his supposed good fortune by intermittent drinking of the takings. The inevitable result was the collapse of the club's finances, followed by its closure.

As a result the enterprise of William Goldberg and his friend, Ernest Wells, the Star was not long in being resurrected as the Pelican Club. Little Willie Goldberg gave racing tips in the 'Pink 'Un' under the *nom de course* of 'The Shifter', most of his information being gleaned from the constant haunting of the bars and night clubs of the West End. Ernest Wells, known as 'Swears' from the firm of Swears & Wells, was a genial, asthmatic character, associated with the running of a number of clubs at the turn of the century. Immediately the Star went out of business, these two worthies went hotfoot to York to seek out a wealthy young officer from whom they borrowed the money for the launching of a new club, the name of which was taken from the stuffed pelican on the mantelpiece of the smoking room.

Soon afterwards the Pelican moved into premises in Gerard Street, and an impressive committee was formed under the chairmanship of Sir John Astley, its members including Lord Mandeville (later Duke of Manchester), the Duke of Hamilton, Lord Marcus Beresford and Lord Rossmore. Other members of the club not on the committee besides the Squire, included Sam Lewis and George Edwardes, the impresario.

The thirty-five-year-old Earl of Lonsdale became chairman of the club's boxing committee, on which his brother-in-law, Lord Esme Gordon, and the Squire's cousin by marriage, 'Bay' Middleton, also sat. Because prize-fighting was still illegal, most matches had to be held in the greatest secrecy, but the police turned a blind eye to those at the Pelican Club by reason of the social importance of its members.

In all fights in the club's boxing saloon, the Queensberry Rules were enforced to the letter. Moreover, all barracking by spectators, let alone physical interference, so long a feature of the ringside, was actively discouraged. The Pelican Club came out wholeheartedly for fair play.

In 1885, Jem Smith had won the unofficial championship of all England by defeating Davis in a clandestine match in the cold light of an early December morning on the outskirts of East Grinstead. As Smith was still champion when the Star re-emerged as the Pelican Club, he was enthusiastically adopted by its members, and by none more so than the Squire. While he sparred in their gymnasium, the Pelicans, almost to a man, proclaimed they had a fighter who could beat any American for the heavyweight championship of the world.

Unlike his fellow members, Lord Lonsdale had first-hand knowledge of the standard of boxing in the United States, having spent almost all of 1888 in North America. While in San Francisco, he had seen Peter Jackson, a coloured boy from Australia, fight, and was impressed by 'The Black Diamond' being, in his own words, 'uncommonly good'.

On returning to England in 1889, Lord Lonsdale brought with him an arctic sled with twenty stuffed huskies and a great many more trophies as well as 'The Black Diamond' himself. As soon as they had docked at Southampton, Peter Jackson, whose mild and pleasant manner belied his dynamic ferocity in the ring, was sent to train in secret at Cottesmore, Lord Lonsdale's Leicestershire hunting box.

Back in the Pelican Club, Lord Lonsdale astounded everybody by declaring that he knew a boxer who could beat Jem Smith. An exhibitionist above all things, Lonsdale could never resist making extravagant claims. He had a loathing of betting, which was surprising in so flamboyant a character, but loved to tell a good story, preferably one in which he was the hero. To no small extent, he owed his chairmanship of the boxing committee to his unsubstantiated claim to have beaten John L. Sullivan. To the public he was the 'Yellow Earl', because of the colour of his buttonhole, carriages and servants' livery. To King Edward VII, he was, 'The biggest liar in my kingdom.'

Had they known of the opinion which their future sovereign was to express, most members of the Pelican Club would have agreed that King Edward had the form about right. The idea of their redoubtable Jem Smith being beaten went beyond the point of being preposterous. Sir John Astley even said it was dangerous to put an unknown fighter into the ring with Smith.

While Lord Lonsdale remained smugly aloof, long odds were being asked about Smith, with no one more eager to lay them than the Squire and his cronies. Convinced that their man could beat the champion of the world, they bet as though there were no settling day.

Few events that took place in London that year drew a more fashionable crowd than the match between Jem Smith and the young black fighter on whose behalf the voluble Lord Lonsdale claimed so much. While the police affected complete ignorance of what was afoot, the Pelicans packed a dozen deep around the ringside. There was not much to see, and such as there was reflected no credit on Smith, who had reigned as champion like the one-eyed man in the kingdom of the blind. Matched against a fighter of the superb skill and physique of 'The Black Diamond', he was never in with a chance. By the end of the second round, Smith had taken a beating that he was never to forget, though it was on a disqualification, not a knock-out, that Jackson got the verdict. Blinded by rage as much as the blood from the cuts in his face, Smith realized that he was hopelessly outclassed by the young coloured fighter, and, reverting to type, showed complete disregard for the Queensberry Rules by trying to manhandle his opponent out of the ring.

The Squire was a heavy loser over the fight, but since he was still running through capital at a rate of knots could settle easily enough, so it was his pride rather than his pocket that was hurt. For months the Squire had been taking as close an interest in Smith's training as he had once done in a horse upon whom he was desperate to win. Nothing had been too good for Smith, upon whom he had lavished money with characteristic abandon, treating him to the largest steaks to be had in the West End, the best wine and anything else he wanted. The Squire may not have got much pleasure from Jack Watts riding him a Derby winner, but such was the difference in his attitude to boxing, he was fully prepared to bathe in what he would have regarded as the reflected glory of Smith. When that glory was so badly mauled and battered that there was not even a shred of it left by the end of two rounds, the Squire was amazed, disappointed and very, very angry.

Whereas the Squire could afford the financial losses, even if he did not like them, many other of the Pelicans found it impossible to pay their bets and were, temporarily at least, disenchanted with the need for enforcing the Queensberry Rules. They wanted their money back as badly as the Squire yearned for the restoration of the prestige of his protégé. A return match being out of the question, they persuaded the club's matchmaker, John Flemming, to arrange a fight between Jem Smith and another Australian, this time a white one, Frank Paddy Slavin. Billed as 'The Sydney Cornstalk', Slavin was an experienced fighter of great ability who had beaten Jake Kilrain in nine rounds at Hoboken, New Jersey, in 1891.

From the outset there were some disturbing aspects to this fight. Despite the blind eye the police turned to what took place in the Pelican Club, this contest was to be staged on the tennis lawn of a retired British army officer living on the outskirts of Bruges, the capital of the Belgian province of West Flanders. Meanwhile the Squire and his henchmen were betting still more heavily than before, and, ominously, they were not backing Smith to win. Instead, they were betting that he would not lose.

As soon as Frank Paddy Slavin reached the ringside, he must have known that his skill was not going to be allowed to avail him anything. In his corner he and his seconds were quite alone. On the other side of the tennis court, Jem Smith was surrounded by the Squire and all the most disreputable elements of the Pelican Club. Still more ominously, the Squire had an even heavier escort than usual, the unprepossessing members of which were armed with truncheons, coshes, knuckledusters and, in one case, a revolver.

Quite undeterred by that grim sight, 'The Sidney Cornstalk' fought as hard as he had done against Kilrain in the United States. Although not able to dominate Smith with the contemptuous ease that Peter Jackson had done, he had established the upper hand by about the half-way stage of the fight. Seeing that the desired result was highly unlikely to materialize, the Squire rose unsteadily to his feet just before the end of the fifteenth round, his face more flushed by extreme displeasure than the champagne he had been drinking all day, and, staggering into the ring, rallied his followers with the stirring exhortation to, 'Do in the Australian Bastard.'

Thereupon the fray was entered by Lord Mandeville and a handful of like-minded sportsmen who were more concerned with abstract ideas of fair play than the practicalities of securing an outcome pleasing to the Squire. Having interpreted the strange features of the betting correctly, and suspecting something very fishy afoot, Lord Mandeville had prudently come equipped with a Bowie knife. Confronted by that formidable armament, the flower of the Squire's chivalry broke ranks and fled, knobkerries, knuckledusters, revolver and all. Well to their rear came their paymaster, with his rapidity of movement greatly impaired by his advanced state of intoxication.

As the match had been stopped by a factor other than the intervention of the referee, it had to be declared a draw, so the Squire and his associates won their bets.

Thus it was that the prospects of prize-fighting attaining legality and recognition were severely damaged by a drunken brawl on a tennis court in Flanders.

When news of the 'Affair at Bruges', as it came to be known, reached London, Sir John Astley summoned a meeting of the committee of the Pelican Club. Little investigation being needed to prove that the Squire had stood the whole racket by defraying the cost of the interventionist party, he was promptly expelled from the club. Rather than accept verdict and sentence, he overcame his habitual horror of litigation by asking the Court of Chancery to declare his expulsion illegal. The law was not that much of an ass.

As things fell out, the Squire came off none the worse from the 'Affair at Bruges'. Expulsion from the Pelican Club was no more than an empty gesture by its committee, the last flicker of life in a dying body. The fracas in Belgium, in which so many of its members, and even its matchmaker, were involved, completely ruined its credibility as a body capable of enforcing the Queensberry Rules, and it was wound up soon afterwards. Eventually, what had been first the Star Club, then the Pelican Club, was revived yet again in its enduring guise as the National Sporting Club as a consequence of the indefatigable efforts of Lord Lonsdale.

After the 'Affair at Bruges', the Squire started to lose interest in racing and riding as he settled down to enjoy the pleasures of London and the *demi-monde*. For company he still chose Charlie Mitchell and the other fighting men, the ladies of the town and the proliferation of self-styled secretaries for whose imaginary services he paid so handsomely, both voluntarily and involuntarily.

The Squire had developed an immense, and almost touching, confidence in Charlie Mitchell. It was not only upon the other's brawn that he was becoming increasingly reliant, but on what he saw as the cockney pugilist's sagacity. In the conduct of his colourfully variegated social life, the Squire took few decisions without due consultation with Mitchell, who was now his bodyguard-in-chief, major-domo, pander and, when the degree of his patron's inebriation demanded it, nursemaid. In his maudlin moments, of which there were not a few, he was wont to tell the older man, 'Charlie, when I die I'm going to leave everything to you.'

Whatever defects there may have been in the character of Charlie Mitchell, and they were multitudinous, there was no doubting his courage. Although no more than a cruiser weight, he never shrank from encounter with a heavyweight, and on becoming the unofficial British champion, went to the United States to fight John L. Sullivan in Madison Square Garden, New York, on 14th May 1883. Having been knocked out of the ring in the second round, he went down in the third, and though he made to get up, Captain Williams of the New York City Police intervened to save him from further punishment.

Despite his having failed to go anything like the distance with 'The Boston Strong Boy', Charlie Mitchell fought him again on 10th March 1888 when they met in Europe on the gallops of Baron de Rothschild's private stable in the Forest of Chantilly. A far stronger and more mature fighter than he had been five years previously, Mitchell put up a superb performance that must have amazed the American camp. After thirty rounds he was still giving as good as he got from Sullivan, and at the end of the thirty-ninth their seconds called it a draw.

Charlie Mitchell, who married a daughter of Pony Moore of the once famous Moore and Burgess Minstrels, revealed immense ingenuity in producing specious pretexts for extracting money from the Squire, a highly developed art in which he was excelled only by the suave and urbane 'Stiffy' Smith. By and large he looked after his money well, investing much of it in property in the Hove area, but, once on a racecourse, he was nothing more than a mug punter, even when he had his card marked by his friend Charlie Hannam, the most astute professional backer of that era. T. H. Dey, founder of the firm still represented on the rails, was always happy to oblige by laying him over the odds and never even bothered to hedge the boxer's bets. It was nothing for Mitchell to have £60 to £10 about the horse for which he had a tip, five each way his own fancy, a bit on the favourite and then a saver on an outsider at the off! Even when he managed to back the winner, he was as often as not still a loser on the race.

In some ways, Charlie Mitchell was really rather an amusing rogue. Once he undertook to collect £50 which a publican at Black Rock, Brighton, owed a bookmaker on the understanding they would go halves if the bet were recovered. In due course the bookmaker asked what success he had had.

'Oh! I got my half,' said Charlie quite casually, 'but I couldn't get yours.'

Another member of the Squire's entourage in those last days of his life was the veteran James Mace. There must have something pathetic about Jem Mace, once the pride of the British ring, fawning on the Squire in late middle age.

Originally a cabinet-maker by trade, Jem Mace had been born at Beeston in Norfolk in 1831. When he began to make a name for himself in the boxing booths around the country fairs, they billed him as 'The Swaffham Gypsy', despite his protesting that he did not have a drop of Romany blood in him, and on 18th June 1861, three months before the birth of the Squire, he became heavyweight champion of Britain. In that dark age of boxing, no other fighter did more, either by example or talent, to restore it to the status of Noble Art that it had enjoyed during the Augustan age. Whenever possible, he wore gloves, and was in no small part instrumental in their introduction.

Although he may have been seduced by the luxury of life in the West End, Jem Mace was neither a ruffian nor a layabout at heart. More than likely he tried to exert a moderating influence on the Squire, but by the second half of 1892 that was beginning to be a singularly unproductive exercise.

16 EXIT CHARLIE MORTON

AS the Gay 'Nineties got under way during the winter of 1890–91, the Squire whooped it up with greater fervour than ever before, while willingly footing the bill for all who would bear him company in his escapades around the West End. By this time, though, even some sections of not very polite society were beginning to look askance at the alcholic antics of the millionaire hedonist.

Any falling off which there may have been in the following he had had in his jollifications of the previous winter would have passed altogether unnoticed by the Squire since Charlie Mitchell, his self-appointed Master of the Revels, and the rest of the fighting men made sure that he was never for a moment at a loss for amusement. Yet, as the opening of the 1891 flat racing season drew closer, he could still just occasionally pull himself away from the pleasures of the metropolis in order to make the journey to Newmarket to see the horses at Bedford Lodge and ride them work.

Among the older horses still in the yard was Quartus, who was responding to the skilful handling of Charlie Morton by showing signs of becoming a reformed character in that spring of 1891, and even gave an earnest of his good intentions by winning the opening race of the season in the hands of Fred Barrett at Lincoln. The Squire also won the second race with Despot, ridden by George Barrett, and on the third day showed that he could still ride after his winter's roistering by getting Everywhere home by a short head in the seller.

Making the traditional journey to Liverpool in the second half of the week, he won on Tommy Tittlemouse, owned by J. T. Whipp, a bookmaker who trained a few of his own horses at Beverley, and saw Lady Rosebery win the Liverpool Spring Cup. At Hurst Park he won on Rullianus, and then at Windsor on Montaigne.

Those four winners in three weeks completely restored the Squire's enthusiasm for race riding, and the weekend before the Epsom spring meeting he said to Morton, 'I'd like to ride a winner at Epsom. I have never had any luck there. Do you think we've got anything on which I could win? Have you got a horse that could win a race of any sort?'

In those days there were races called overnight handicaps, such as Epsom's Tadworth Stakes, which closed on Monday night, the weights being published on Tuesday before running on Wednesday. The six furlongs of that event were just the distance for Juggler.

'There's Juggler,' said Morton in reply to the Squire's question. 'I could put him in the Tadworth Stakes. He is certain to get a big weight. They are only a moderate lot in these races that close overnight. You can do the weight for him all right, but whether you will win on him is another matter.'

Most administrative duties at Epsom, including the handicapping, were undertaken by Mr H. M. Dorling, a long-standing friend of Morton who said to him, 'Now, Mr Dorling, I've got a horse here, and the Squire is very anxious to ride it. You know what a supporter of your meeting he is, and he is very keen to ride a winner here. I've put Juggler in an overnight handicap and I want you to do me a good turn and give him the best chance you can.'

Dorling said he would see what he could do, and, as good as his word, gave Juggler 10 stone with the others too little below him to have any chance on known form.

The Squire habitually bemoaned his luck at Epsom, where he had ridden only one more winner since Tommy Upton in 1886. That was on Charleston, who beat a filly called Lady Onslow at the spring meeting of 1888. By the time he jumped up on Juggler, he had had another winner there as he rode The Rejected to beat George Chaloner on Versifier by a head, and then survived an objection for bumping on the Tuesday.

The following afternoon the ring went 6/1 bar one and asked for 11/8 Juggler in the opening race. Despite him seeming such a good thing, Juggler was never there with any sort of chance and finished unplaced.

As Juggler was being unsaddled, an incredulous Morton asked what had happened. 'Nothing,' said the Squire. 'He would not go at all.' And then, with the perversity that is the perogative of millionaires and madmen, added, 'Don't let him run any more.'

Vainly Morton remonstrated against retiring a horse still in his prime. The Squire, however, furious with frustration, was quite immune to reason.

'Maybe he can win plenty of races,' he said sulkily as he went back into the weighing room to change into different colours, 'but I don't want him to run again. If I can't win on him no one else will. Send him to stud.' So it was that Juggler joined Merry Hampton at the Kentford Stud, where he stood at 25 guineas.

The Squire's humour must have improved later in the afternoon when he won yet another race on The Rejected, who gave a three-year-old, ridden by George Barrett, 39 pounds and a beating of a neck in the Epsom Spring Cup.

Just under a fortnight later, the Squire was again on The Rejected in the Somersetshire Stakes at Bath. In the opinion of many observers, he rode the race of his life that day. Notwithstanding all the harm he had already done his constitution by wasting and dissipation, he found immense reserves of strength with which to drive his mount up to beat Mounteagle by half a length. He then went on to complete a double on Bob Armstrong's Pierrepont.

Going to Salisbury at the end of that week, the Squire continued to ride as well as ever. In the first three races of the first day, he brought off a treble by beating a professional jockey in each of them, and was only beaten a head on his other mount that afternoon. For the second of those winners, Lord Dudley's Orange Peel, the horse against which he had ridden that memorable deadheat at Liverpool, he weighed out at only 9 stone 10 pounds. The following day he won on The Rejected for the fourth time that season.

The ordeal of getting down to 9 stone 10 pounds must have been most unpleasant for a man of the age and height of the Squire. Although it was still only spring, he was riding at two pounds less than he had the previous summer, the time at which jockeys are at their lowest natural weight. Such intensive reduction can have done his health no good, but it did show that his will-power was still strong.

Meanwhile the reformation of Quartus was proving no more than temporary. Following the success at Lincoln, the Squire himself rode his £6,000 purchase at Windsor later in March, but though the horse started 11/8 favourite, the best that he could do was to finish third of four. At long last Charlie Morton was to have his chance to be rid of the horse, who was promptly entered for the Two Thousand Guineas Trial Plate at Newmarket on 28th April. That event was only a seller, the winner of which was to be sold for £2,000 unless an allowance was claimed by entering for less, a condition of which Morton took full advantage by putting the wretched Quartus in with a price tag of £500.

As much to the surprise as the relief of Morton, Quartus won, and won impressively. At the subsequent auction, he was knocked down to a bid of 1,020 guineas from a man called Deacon, whose horses were trained by Jimmy Waugh at Meynell House (now Hurworth House), Newmarket.

Later that afternoon, Bob Peck said to Charlie Morton, 'You've done a clever thing. You have let a damned good horse go.' Even more convinced of the folly of Morton and the excellence of Quartus was Jimmy Waugh. In the autumn, tangible proof of that good opinion was seen when the big chestnut was backed down from 33/1 to 10/1 favourite for the Cambridgeshire.

Bob Lee, one of the leading bookmakers, sought out Morton and said, 'There's a lot of money for that horse you used to have. I am told he will win the Cambridgeshire.'

'Are you?' replied Morton. 'Well, I know he won't.'

That night Jimmy Waugh, having heard of what Morton had been saying, came round to Bedford Lodge in a state of some perturbation. 'I think he will win,' he said. 'I haven't tried him yet, but I shall be very much mistaken if he does not do what I ask him. I'm going to try him tomorrow and I'll let you know what happens.'

'You needn't bother to tell me,' said Morton laconically.

When they were out with their strings at second lot the following day, Jimmy Waugh hacked over to Morton to say, 'By jove, you were right. I've tried the brute and he is not worth a shilling. I have never been so mistaken about a horse in my life.'

'Yes,' said Morton, 'I know. I've had some.'

After that trial, Quartus took a long walk out to 40/1 in the betting on the Cambridgeshire, in which he ran unplaced to Comedy. And that, to all intents and purposes, was the end of the story of the Squire's £6,000 horse.

The week after Quartus had won at Newmarket, the Squire brought off a double on Boom, running in the name of William Stevens, and William Sibary's Delaval on the first day of the Kempton Park Jubilee meeting, and throughout the late spring and early summer he continued to ride winners. In the middle of July he went north to Scotland again to ride at Hamilton Park, that pleasant course eleven miles from Glasgow, the city wherein lay the origin of the great fortune he had been spending so freely for more than a decade.

The Hamilton Park course had been laid out under the supervision of Sir John Astley, while that most amiable but most impecunious of baronets had been put up in great splendour at the near-by ducal palace in 1887. The inaugural meeting, well supported by the Baird family, the Duke of Montrose and other prominent Scottish owners, had been held in July 1888 when both the Squire's runners were unplaced and Douglas Baird won with Barskimming.

At the Hamilton Park meeting three years later in the middle of July 1891, the Squire won on Captain Cameron's Patchouli. On his only other mount, Alf Day's Primus, he was second beaten three lengths by the six-year-old Commissary, owned by a Mr Robert Hayward. At a subsequent inquiry, the stewards found that the correct age of Commissary had not been given at entry, and as well as disqualifying him in favour of Primus, reported the matter to the stewards of the Jockey Club. They heard the case at Goodwood on 29th July and had recourse to the ultimate sanction of warning off Robert Hayward, a punishment that seems excessively severe for what was hardly more than a technical offence, especially as Commissary was a well-known horse and a winner at Thirsk two months previously. Presumably there was a lot more to this affair than meets the eye.

Also before the stewards who handed out such apparently harsh justice to Robert Hayward at Goodwood was a case in which the Squire was still more closely involved. This had arisen out of the running of the Warrington Welter Plate at Liverpool on 21st July. For that event, Bob Armstrong, the Penrith trainer, ran both the 6/5 on favourite Lux, ridden by the Squire, and the 100/14 outsider of three, Cordon Bleu, with Freddie Rickaby up. The other runner was the 11/8 chance Dainty Davie, the mount of Johnnie Osborne, 'The Old Pusher', as his fellow northerners dubbed that unstylish but singularly effective veteran.

Contrary to what had been suggested by the betting, Cordon Bleu came out the better of the Armstrong pair, beating Dainty Davie by a length. Three lengths away trailed the Squire on the odds-on chance.

'The attention of the Stewards,' in the official words of the *Racing Calendar*, 'having been drawn to the running of Mr Armstrong's horses', they interviewed the Squire, Freddie Rickaby and Bob Armstrong, and not being satisfied with their explanation, referred the case to the stewards of the Jockey Club. Having held their preliminary inquiry at Goodwood, the club's stewards, Prince Soltykoff, a Russian nobleman of more than twenty years residence in England, Mr J. Houldsworth and Lord Durham, adjourned the case until the Newmarket Houghton meeting.

At the resumed hearing, the stewards came to the conclusion that there was not 'sufficient evidence forthcoming to enable them to take further steps in the matter' – a verdict of 'Not guilty' delivered with singular reluctance, and the more unflattering in that it was preceeded by the words, 'though there were gravely suspicious circumstances connected with the case'.

The defeats of odds-on favourites like Lux at Liverpool and Juggler at Epsom provided welcome ammunition for those convinced that the Squire was the biggest villain who ever rode a horse. Despite the enormous success he had enjoyed in the late 1880s, his army of detractors still contained those who insisted that he was in the pay of the bookmakers, a quaint theory that was as much confounded by his obsession with riding winners as it was by his not needing to be paid by anyone. The only way in which he jeopardized the interests of punters was by riding when he was drunk, and that, by the summer of 1891, was becoming somewhat frequent.

Whoever gave the most heartfelt sigh of relief when the stewards of the Jockey Club eventually announced their far from unequivocal verdict at Newmarket, it was not the Squire. To be involved in any scandal without being the principal culprit was an almost novel experience for him. It might even have been a refreshing one, had he not almost reached the stage at which he was beyond being refreshed by touches of irony or anything else.

On the same day that he was beaten on Lux at Liverpool, the Squire won on J. T. Whipp's St Crispin, who brought his score to the first half of the season to twenty-one. During the second half he rode just five winners. On William the Silent, owned and trained by Joe Cannon, he won at both Huntingdon and Derby, on Niagara at Hungtingdon and on Upset at Derby. Finally he returned to Derby to obtain another success on Tommy Tittlemouse in the middle of November.

The old, overpowering passion to ride winners anywhere and everywhere was cooling fast. Still worse, his nerve was going. The bold words spoken over brandy late and long into the night were no longer translated into some semblance of action when he reached the course on the morrow. His happiest thoughts were coming in the form of memories – memories of hard-fought finishes ridden against such masters of their trade as Cannon, Watts and Webb, finishes of which any Gentleman Rider could be proud without needing a crowd of the greediest and most dishonest scroungers in the country to shower him with its worthless praise.

All through the winter of 1891–2 he drank still harder than he done during the previous one. And when, in late February, it was time to go back to Newmarket to ride the early runners in their trials and gallops, he remained in London for the joy of hearing his praises sung by Charlie Mitchell, Jem Smith and the rest of the gang. Even when he could hardly sit straight on a chair, let alone stand, they were telling him that he could throw a harder punch than a man half his weight again.

Meanwhile, Charlie Morton, his letters unanswered, carried on as best he could in the service of his 'revered employer' at Bedford Lodge. Training for the Squire was becoming impossible, in circumstances that were so very different from what they had been out the outset of their association four years earlier when the young millionaire had been as dedicated to race riding as any apprentice from the slums of the Midlands or the North.

As the days grew longer and warmer and the spring of 1892 drew nearer to summer, the closer the Squire drove Charlie Morton to despair. Bedford Lodge became something like a stable in quarantine, with none of its inmates allowed to run. The Squire did not want to have runners unless he was going to ride a winner at the meeting, but was never available to ride as he was always being taken off to a gymnasium to see some fighter in training or to fulfil some other specious engagement invented by Charlie Mitchell, or he was just plain drunk.

Charlie Morton had the horses fit, well and ready to run, all to no avail. Even when he got them as far as the course, a henchman would come along to tell him that the Squire did not want any of his horses to run that day.

Matters came to a head at Epsom on 31st May 1892, by which stage of the season the Squire had not ridden a winner from the very few mounts that he had taken. Just as Morny Cannon was about to weigh out to ride King of Diamonds in the five-furlong Egmont Handicap, one of those uncouth errand boys came up to Morton, saying, 'I have just left the Squire and he says that he does not want to run King of Diamonds.'

At last Charlie Morton had reached the limit of his patience. On four previous occasions within the weeks preceeding the Derby meeting he had brought King of Diamonds to the course, and each time had been instructed to take him home again.

'I don't care,' snapped Morton, thoroughly exasperated. 'The horse is going to run.' And he did, beating Cloudberry by a head. Then, just for good measure, Morton brought King of Diamonds out two days later on the Thursday, when he beat the same horse by a neck. The most immediate loser by Morton's open defiance of the Squire was Cloudberry's owner, Colonel Oliver Montagu, a younger son of Lord Sandwich. The Colonel was Equerry to the Prince of Wales and devoted friend, in an utterly platonic way, of the frequently abandoned Princess of Wales.

Rather than be pleased by having won two races at one of the most fashionable meetings of the season, the Squire seethed with anger at Morton having ignored his fatuous orders. When two of his gloating cronies conveyed in detail the full extent of his displeasure, Morton took the ground from under their feet by saying, 'Then he had better get another trainer.'

Lillie Langtry tried to effect a reconciliation between the Squire and his trainer. That lady, who never did very much in a spirit of altruism, had her own reason for wanting to see no changes in management at Bedford Lodge. Milford, one of the two-year-olds the Squire had given her, had won at Kempton Park first time out and was coming on as though he might win again at Ascot. A change of trainers could affect the colt's chances at the Royal Meeting, or he could even be left with no trainer at all.

In the face of all the charm and persuasion of the beautiful Mrs Langtry, Charlie Morton remained unmoved. After four years of dramas and vicissitudes at Bedford Lodge he had had more than he could stand. The fickleness of the Squire, which all too often impinged upon the work of the trainer, was bad enough, but that of his mannerless, arrogant hangers-on, who knew nothing about horses for all their airs and expertise, had become as perfectly intolerable to him as it had to Martin Gurry five years earlier. To save the Squire's face a statement was put out that Charlie Morton was retiring from training for a while because of poor health.

The career of King of Diamonds, the horse that figured in the final rift between the Squire and his second private trainer, came to an unexpected end. Shortly after the departure of Morton he and Snaplock, the big chestnut stayer, got loose on the Limekilns. While George Lambton and others looked on without being close enough to intervene, the pair of them began fighting. With Snaplock getting the upper hand, King of Diamonds fled up the gallop and along the Bury Road towards Bedford Lodge with Snaplock in pursuit and Jack Watts giving chase on his hack. As Snaplock was too close on the heels of King of Diamonds to allow him to lose ground by making the turn into the stableyard, they careered on past the newly erected Jubilee clock, through the town to the Rowley Mile stands where they came to grips again and a running fight ensued until they broke off from exhaustion close to the Cesarewitch start.

Neither horse was ever good again. Rather curiously, both were to fetch the same price, 310 guineas, at the dispersal sale of the Squire's horses.

17 DOWNHILL

THE difficulty that the Squire had experienced in finding a private trainer after his final rupture with 'Smush' Gurry in the summer of 1888 was nothing more than a slight complication compared to that which he met when trying to find a successor to Charlie Morton in 1892. By that time he was thirty years of age, in a steadily advancing state of inebriation and so completely under the influence of the prize-fighters that he was taking very little interest in racing and riding.

As he spent so much of his time hanging around the boxing saloons and gymnasiums when he was not tippling in Romano's or making a nuisance of himself in some other place of public refreshment, the Squire saw very little of the racing fraternity. One of the few members of it whom he still met regularly, however, was Tom Cannon's younger brother Joe, who was also an ardent follower of the fight game. Almost as fine a horseman as Tom, but a good deal heavier, Joe had been obliged to turn to steeplechasing and had won the Grand National on Regal in 1876. Where this pleasant, easy-going man differed from his more famous brother was in his inability to handle money, a commodity of which he was generally in very short supply. In consequence, he was reliant upon a series of jobs as private trainer until eventually able to open a stable of his own. For a time he had trained for Captain Machell, whose colours he had worn on Regal, at Bedford Cottage, and been responsible for Pilgrimage, owned by Lord Lonsdale's elder brother St John, the 4th Earl, winning the Two Thousand Guineas and the One Thousand Guineas in 1878. Later he was private trainer to Lord Rosebery, for whom he brought off the double with Vista in the Great Metropolitan and Roisterer in the City and Suburban at Epsom in 1883.

In addition to training the horses of whoever might be his patron for the time being, Joe Cannon usually had one or two moderate animals of his own. It was on one of these, William the Silent, a five-year-old by Robert the Devil, as already mentioned, that he had provided the Squire with winning rides at Huntingdon and Derby in the late summer of 1891. By doing so, Joe Cannon had raised himself in the estimation of the Squire in much the same way as Charlie Morton had done by giving him the mount on Bismarck at Windsor in 1888. Therefore it was only natural that, in his desperation to find another trainer, the Squire should turn to a fellow fight fan to whom he was already so well disposed, and who was, in addition, the brother of his first trainer.

Joe Cannon was as wary of accepting the Squire's offer, generous though it was, as Charlie Morton had been four years previously. Contrary to what had been the case with Morton, though, he was not already engaged in running a successful stable of his own, so, resolving to stand no nonsense from the Squire, nor interference from his friends, he agreed to take over the Bedford Lodge yard.

Seven years had passed since the Squire had ceased to be a disqualified person. In each of these years he had finished at the top of the list of winning Gentlemen Riders on the flat, but only now, when his interest was waning and his nerve impaired by more than one crashing fall while he was drinking more heavily than ever, did his investment in racing reach its fullest. Early in 1892 he purchased from Lord Gerard the Moulton Paddocks stud, which lies just beyond the brow of Warren Hill on the road running from Newmarket to Moulton, and, taking Merry Hampton and Busybody and the other mares from the stud that he had rented from Captain Machell at Kentford, he installed them all there.

Although Joe Cannon was training the horses at Bedford Lodge, and Jugg, who had charge of the Kentford stud, had moved into Moulton Paddocks, the overall management of the Squire's greatly expanded racing interests was vested in the former jockey, Charles Morbey. That remarkably shrewd individual had been apprenticed to Peter Price, who had the Somerville Lodge stable on Newmarket's Fordham Road, and had obtained his first important success by riding Lord Rosebery's Aldritch at 6 stone 4 pounds to win the City and Suburban as a boy of eighteen in 1874. Subsequently he made a lot of money riding for the

Nottingham bookmaker, Charlie Hibbert, who was never averse to deserting his calling by backing his runners heavily. Of the forty-seven winners that Morbey rode in 1881, one of the most successful seasons of his career, sixteen, or almost exactly a third, were owned by Hibbert.

Having achieved prosperity, Charlie Morbey bought a lot of agricultural land and other property in the village of Soham, a few miles from Newmarket. Among the houses that he owned there was Beechurst, which is now the school, and his own home, the Moat, while his wife owned Addison House.

It was at the Moat that Charlie Morbey played the genial host by giving card parties for the especial delight of the Squire and the members of those singularly unrefined house parties at Bedford Lodge. The further into the night they drank and the thicker the room became with cigar smoke, the more these ruffians told the Squire what a good sport he was and how his luck was bound to turn soon while making good and sure that it did nothing of the sort.

The resourceful Charlie Morbey was rarely at a loss to know how to deal with the Squire, whose eccentricities included a periodic aversion to signing cheques, a legacy, perhaps, from the days of his minority when he had so rarely had any money in his current account at the Strand branch of Coutts. On Morbey asking him for a cheque to cover stable expenses one day, the Squire rummaged around his desk and then declared, 'I can't find a pen.'

'I've thought of that,' said Morbey, producing one from his waistcoat pocket, whereupon the Squire countered him by knocking over the inkstand.

'Oh! I've thought of that too, Squire,' said the ex-jockey, and promptly pulled a penny bottle of ink out of his jacket.

Fortunately for the Squire, the change of trainers at Bedford Lodge in mid-season had no adverse effect upon the horses. Milford, whom Morton had saddled to win the £2,400 Royal Plate at Kempton Park a fortnight or so before his departure, continued to work like a high-class horse in the making. Reappearing at Royal Ascot, where he was ridden by Jack Watts, Milford started at 7/4 on in the Coventry Stakes and beat the French colt Marly by a neck.

After the race, Lillie Langtry was offered 20,000 guineas for Milford, a truly enormous price in those days when 5,500 guineas was still a record for a yearling, but, for once, her highly developed mercenary instincts gave way to others and, blinded by the vision of being the first woman to own a Derby winner, she refused to sell. A fortnight later the vision became still brighter when Milford went on to win the July Stakes at Newmarket.

Meanwhile another of the Bedford Lodge two-year-olds was shaping up as though he might make a classic horse the following season. This was the Squire's bay colt, Meddler, the third living foal and first colt from his One Thousand Guineas and Oaks winner, Busybody. The sire of this well-named individual was St Gatien, who had run a dead heat with Harvester in the Derby two days before Busybody had won the Oaks.

As St Gatien had enjoyed little popularity with breeders, he covered few other mares of the quality of Busybody before being exported to Germany in 1890. He probably owed his mating with Busybody to the foresight of his owner, that remarkable character, Jack Hammond, who had started life as a stable lad when Joe Dawson had trained at Bedford Lodge and made his way up in the world by clever betting. Appreciating the benefits that might accrue from cultivating the Squire, Jack Hammond had taken care to provide him with a few fancied rides like Strathblane who had won at Warwick in late November 1886.

Ten days after Milford had won at Royal Ascot, Meddler made his début in the £1,000 British Dominion Plate, confined to horses bred and trained within the dominions of the Crown, at Sandown Park. As anything that happened in the Squire's stable was bound to be bruited, in varying degrees of inaccuracy and exaggeration, all over London, the colt's reputation had preceeded him by a very long way. Consequently the ring asked 4/1 about him, a price that he readily justified. With George Barrett in the saddle, he beat Colonel North's filly Emita by three lengths. The following month, when he was ridden by Morny Cannon, Meddler won again by beating the Duke of Portland's Kilmarnock by the same margin in the Chesterfield Stakes at the Newmarket second July meeting.

Although he had bred two of the season's outstanding two-year-olds, and owned one of them, the Squire was still taking little or no interest in racing. Instead, he continued to lurk in London, passing his days in the more disreputable dives. For all that they tried, neither Joe Cannon nor Charlie Morbey could find ways of wheedling him away from the company of the fighting men to come back to Newmarket.

The Squire hardly rode a gallop during the spring and early summer of 1892, and scarcely took a mount in public at all. It was not until 21st June that he obtained his first success of the season, though through no more difficult a process than walking over for the Rothschild Plate at

Windsor on Quebec, owned by the well-known commission agent Teddy Hobson, who was to win the Cesarewitch with Burnaby in the autumn. Gone were the days when the Squire paid huge sums of money to any owner or trainer who would start a horse against him to make a race of it.

On the second day of that Windsor meeting in June 1892, the Squire won a second race in almost as hollow a manner as he had the mount on Lord William Beresford's Catarina in the Eton Cup, for horses the property of Old Etonians. Starting at 100/8 on, Catarina won by three lengths from her only rival, Carronade, ridden by twenty-two-year-old Mr George Thursby in the colours of his father Sir John. Although the result is of no importance, and can never have been in much doubt, the race is of some historical interest as it marks the overlapping of the careers of two of the greatest of all amateur riders on the flat.

George Thursby did not win his first race under Jockey Club rules until he rode Foghorn in the Bibury Stakes at Stockbridge early the following month, but long after the death of the Squire he was to develop into a finer race rider than most of the professionals of his day, and is the only amateur to have been placed in the Derby. As already mentioned, he was second on John O'Gaunt in 1904 and third on Picton in 1906. He rode his last winner a few weeks before his fiftieth birthday in 1919, and the following year succeeded his half-brother as 3rd Baronet. He died at the age of seventy-one in 1941.

If, as would have been characteristic of him, Lord William Beresford gave the Squire the mount of Catarina in the hope of rekindling his enthusiasm for race riding, his generosity was of no avail. More than the filip of riding an easy winner was needed. He was making spasmodic attempts to resume riding seriously, but the will was becoming as weak as the flesh. The flame that Fred Archer and Tom Cannon had lit was guttering out.

Following the walk-over and almost equally effortless winning ride in that match at Windsor, the Squire proceeded to obtain his third success of the season without his waning powers being put to the test either. Riding Harry Heasman's Ellerton at Hurst Park in July, he was beaten three parts of a length by Walter Bradford on William Stevens's Little Tich, who was disqualified for boring and cannoning. The stewards exonerated Bradford from all blame. They might have been rather more suspicious about how the runner-up came to meet with sufficient interference to warrant his being given the race had they known of the full extent of the involvement of William Stevens with the Squire. Just as much as Joe

Cannon, Stevens needed to reawaken the Squire's enthusiasm for racing.

In the early autumn the Squire managed to drag himself away from the brothels and pot-houses of London to pay his annual visit to Scotland. By this time his life-style, with its almost total indifference to normal nutrients of the solid variety, was beginning to take as heavy a toll of his body as it had already done his mind. Consequently he could, without any effort whatever, go to the scales at a weight pounds below that which he had tortured himself with starvation to do when at the zenith of his powers as a rider.

On 30th September 1892, he celebrated his thirty-first and, as things fell out, his last birthday by getting himself the ride on Mr H. M. Dyas's bay mare Alice in the Edinburgh Gold at Musselburgh at what must have been enormous expense. As Alice had won the Ebor Handicap the previous month and the Ayreshire Handicap at the Western Meeting earlier in the current month, while her only opponent, Lord Rosebery's Accumulator, was a maiden three-year-old, she was the certainty of the season despite the enfeebled condition of her rider, who weighed out at a mere 9 stone 5 pounds.

Had there been a set-to at the end of the two miles, Alice would have had no help at all from the saddle. As it was, though, none was needed as she beat Accumulator, ridden by George Manser, by two lengths at 8/1 on to make the Squire's last mount in his own country a winning one.

Back in England the following month, the Squire rode his last winner of all under Jockey Club rules on his own colt Porridge, a chestnut out of Oatflake, at Gatwick on 18th October, when he beat Ben Loates on Mr Leopold de Rothschild's Bumptious by a neck in a field of four for the six-furlong Montefiore Stakes. It was not much of a swan song, but at least the race took a bit more winning than the other four which had fallen to his lot that season.

Meanwhile Meddler was proving himself a worthy descendant of the great mares that had once been part of Lord Falmouth's priceless Mereworth Stud. Reappearing in the Dewhurst Plate with Morny Cannon up at Newmarket on 27th September, Meddler beat the Duke of Portland's Raeburn by three parts of a length with Lord Calthorpe's Buckingham a head away third and Douglas Baird's Harbinger last of four.

The Dewhurst form was good. Raeburn had won the Ham Stakes at Goodwood and then the Boscawen Stakes at Newmarket, before being a fair fourth to Colonel Harry McCalmont's Isinglass, the champion two-year-old of the season, in the Middle Park Plate. The implication was therefore that Meddler only had to make a bit more than average improvement from two to three years of age to have a chance of beating Isinglass in the Derby.

Perhaps it was because he was no longer an almost first-class race rider, or it may have on account of his having bred the colt himself, but the Squire took a good deal more pleasure in the triumphs of Meddler than he had in that of Merry Hampton in the Derby. Pride in ownership of the horse made him resolve to take his racing seriously again, and he confided to George Lambton and Arthur Coventry, once the most formidable of his rivals in the races confined to Gentlemen Riders, that he was cutting loose from the fighting men who had fed upon his bounty for so long. After it had seemed impossible that he could ever do anything of the sort, he was beginning to see how near he had been brought to mental, moral, physical and even financial ruin by false friends who wanted nothing of him save his money.

In early November, about a fortnight after the success of Meddler in the Dewhurst, the Squire gave some evidence of the seriousness of his intention to refashion his life by going north to Liverpool, where he took three mounts at the autumn meeting at Aintree. On the Thursday he was third on William Sibary's Delaval, beaten just three parts of a length and a neck by Ben Loates on Romeo and Jim Fagan on Buillon, and later in the afternoon he finished in the same place on Tommy Tittlemouse. Tommy Tittlemouse was brought out again for the Members' Welter Handicap for Gentlemen Riders on the Saturday when the Squire deserted him for Junius, who started 13/8 favourite on the strength of his having been a good second at the York August meeting. This time York form did not work as satisfactorily as it had done in the case of Alice, since Junius could only finish third of four, beaten three lengths and four by Sir Blundell Maple's Grace Darling, ridden by Bob Peck's son Charles.

When the Squire returned to Newmarket, heavier and healthier than he had been for months and looking forward to what Meddler would achieve as a three-year-old, it seemed impossible that he had ridden his last race.

18 THE LAST CHANCE

AT the end of the flat-racing season of 1892, the Squire repaired to the tall, narrow red-brick house almost opposite the more sedate residence of the Earl of Crewe in Curzon Street, in order to spend the winter in London. And how he spent!

Almost every appearance of his pocket-book was greeted by the cheers of his entourage of prize-fighters and other scroungers and getabits as he toured the hotels, restaurants, seedier public houses and brothels. By this time he was making the very minimum effort to exercise any judgment of men, and none at all to curb his absolutely natural generosity. Drinking champagne by the pint to the acclamation of his followers was giving him every bit as much exhilaration as riding winners had done. Meanwhile, requests for 'loans' were met and remuneration to his 'secretaries' was made with largesse on a still grander scale than hitherto.

His high hopes of Meddler for the classics of 1893 and resolution to regain the reputation as the greatest Gentleman Rider in the British Empire were completely forgotten amid the popping of champagne corks. Hardly a day went by without his giving offence by the manner of his salutation to some passer-by in the street or his involvement in some other highly embarrassing scene. Quite one of his favourite japes was to pour a drink over a complete stranger in a restaurant. Any resentment which the act might arouse was speedily and efficiently suppressed by the good offices of Charlie Mitchell or one of the other boys.

In the middle of that winter of 1892–3, Mitchell, 'Stiffy' Smith,

Teddy Bayly, probably the most superfluous of all the Squire's secretaries, and a few others hit upon an idea for redistributing the Baird wealth more widely than ever before. They told their patron it was his destiny to make boxing history by sending Mitchell to the United States to wrest the heavyweight championship of the world from 'Gentleman Jim' Corbett and bring it back to Britain.

Having displayed no pleasure whatever at winning the Derby five years previously, the Squire began to allow himself illusions of grandeur. He saw himself a national hero, receiving the plaudits of the sporting public for underwriting the triumph of Mitchell. Soon the most enterprising of his friends were busy inventing pretexts for drawing money from him to cover the initial expenses of what he was seeing as the most momentous crossing of the Atlantic since Columbus.

In an attempt to set the ball rolling, Charlie Mitchell challenged Corbett to defend his title for a purse of $10,000 to be put up by the Squire. Instead of the ring of steel, the throwing down of this particular gauntlet had the impact of a wet fish on a stone slab. Not a vestige of a reply was received. Perhaps the American's manager, Bill Brady, was unimpressed by the British champion's ignorance of Corbett having temporarily retired from the ring to turn his talents to acting by playing the thinly disguised lead role in a new drama called *Gentleman Jack*.

There was something ironic even about the idea of Mitchell fighting Corbett, as Corbett had done as much to make boxing respectable in America as Mitchell had done to help the Squire to bring it into further disrepute in Britain. As well as being the first champion to introduce tactics and subtlety into pugilism, and using his undoubted intellect to develop his ringcraft, 'Gentleman Jim' had earned his nickname by showing that a boxer could lead an orthodox social life. Thus the former bank clerk refused to be confined to a circle of intimates whose brains were in inverse proportion to their brawn.

One of twelve children of a family of Irish descent, James J. Corbett had been born in San Francisco, California, on 1st September 1866. Having worked for a short time in a bank, he began his career as a professional boxer on a note of anti-climax. Prize-fighting was then illegal in California and police intervened in the fourth round when he met Joe Choynski at Fairfax on 30th May 1889. Five days later, they tried conclusions again on a barge moored off Bernicia, and Corbett was declared the winner after a badly bleeding Choynski withdrew at the end of the twenty-seventh round.

On 18th February 1890, 'Gentleman Jim' established himself as a boxer of national importance by beating Jake Kilrain in New Orleans. Fifteen months later, on 21st May 1891, he amazed the devotees of the fight game by holding Lord Lonsdale's one-time protégé Peter Jackson, 'The Black Diamond', to a draw after sixty-one rounds at the California Athletic Club. That achievement earned him a bid for the championship in a fight with the title-holder, John L. Sullivan.

'The Boston Strong Boy' was eight years older than Corbett, and also of Irish descent, his father having come from Kerry and his mother from Athlone. Sullivan, who had never been able to subject himself to vigorous training at the best of times, was badly out of condition by then and had too little respect for his challenger to do anything about it. Consequently, when they met in New Orleans on 10th March 1892, the faster punching and more agile footwork of Corbett enabled him to dominate the fight, and he won the world championship by knocking out Sullivan in the twenty-first round.

Immediately afterwards, Corbett, who had the boyish good looks of a film star of a later age, took leave of the ring for a while to devote himself to the stage – unknown to Charlie Mitchell. Mitchell's claims to a bid for the world title rested on his having drawn with the previous holder, Sullivan, before the latter had begun to decline, in that fight in France mentioned earlier. Therefore the project to match Mitchell with Corbett was not altogether absurd.

When it became certain that Corbett was going to ignore the challenge from Mitchell, that worthy together with the other architects of the Squire's American venture had to settle for a poor second best as a pretext for the operation. Jem Hall, another of the Squire's fighting circus, was rather hastily matched against the lanky British ex-patriot, Bob Fitzsimmons, in a contest to take place in New Orleans in early March 1893. Fitzsimmons, who had been born at Helston in Cornwall, had been beaten by Hall in just four rounds three years earlier. But whereas 'Fitz' had become a far more polished fighter during the intervening period, Hall had grown gross and flabby in the service of the Squire. According to the revised plans of Mitchell, Bayly and associates, they would take the Squire back to New York after the fight between Hall and Fitzsimmons, when Mitchell would seek out Corbett and challenge him, face to face, to defend the championship.

All the grandiose dreams the Squire had of becoming the patron of the heavyweight champion of the world did nothing to induce him to bring a little order into his life. He still indulged in every kind of riotous, raucous revelry, though the lungs did not bellow as loudly as they had done two or three years earlier amid the regular outbreaks of violence at No. 36 Curzon Street. On one occasion the Squire, Charlie Mitchell and the rest of them were immersed in a game of poker when Chesterfield Goode, a prize-fighter turned bookmaker always recognizable by his white top hat on the race course, and Arthur Coburn, a desperado specializing in knifework, burst in upon them. There was bad blood between Mitchell and Goode, who would dearly have loved to have got his own hands on some of the Squire's money and had more than one score to settle. While Goode lunged at his enemy with his fist, Coburn made to grab the poker, but Mitchell, disengaging the other momentarily, knocked Coburn stone cold, and then, resuming the business in hand, picked up Goode and hurled him down the stairs. That little fracas over, Charlie Mitchell, never too proud to play the nursemaid, carried his hopelessly drunken patron up to bed.

While the Squire's minions cavorted and caroused around Mayfair, his trainer, Joe Cannon, was quite horrified by getting wind of the proposed expedition to the United States. He needed no imagination to envisage what would happen if his employer were to go to a country where recourse was still all too often had to the gun before the law courts. Americans were hardly likely to take kindly to having hats smashed down over their eyes, cigars whipped out of their mouths or the Squire dallying with their wives. Whereas the obliging Charlie Mitchell could always be squared to accept the odd prison sentence, he was hardly likely to be amenable to taking a bullet in the belly, even if he were to be an acceptable proxy. Full of these misgivings, Joe Cannon dashed up to London to try to dissuade the Squire from embarking upon the venture.

On arriving at 36 Curzon Street, Cannon was confronted with a totally unexpected situation. Instead of finding the Squire making lusty whoopee, as had lately been his wont, he met a man in abysmally wretched physical condition, all too obviously paying the penalty of having drunk too much for too long, and deeply depressed. In addition, the Squire was suffering more than ever from the undermining of his health by continual wasting, not least of the consequent ailments being recurrent intestinal trouble. Insufficient nourishment each spring, summer and autumn for close on a decade had lowered his resistance to infection so that he was constantly catching chills which he had great difficulty in shaking off. Still worse, he had been the victim of periodic bouts of pneumonia, and he was still only thirty-one.

The Squire had at last come to the terrifying realization that those he had seen fit to choose as his friends were concerned only with encompassing his destruction. Belatedly he saw that his headlong flight into folly had got hopelessly out of his own control and that someone else would have to apply the brakes before he reached irretrievable personal disaster which would leave him broken in mind and body and, eventually, penniless.

Desperately, he begged Joe Cannon to take him back to Moulton Paddocks so that he could resume the healthy life of a Gentleman Rider. Asked to do the very thing that he had feared might prove quite unacceptable, Cannon willingly agreed to take the Squire back to Newmarket that same evening. First, though, he had to leave the house for an hour or two to attend to some other business, after which he would return with a cab to collect the Squire so that they could travel from Liverpool Street to Newmarket together.

When he returned to 36 Curzon Street, Joe Cannon was first puzzled, and then utterly dismayed, to find that his knocking and ringing of the door-bell elicited no response whatever. The boxers, the bogus secretaries, and the rest of the gang were not going to be baulked of their prey by his racehorse trainer. They had no intention of letting the Squire, and thus, in effect, control of his still substantial fortune, out of their clutches. Eventually, realizing the hopelessness of trying to gain admission to the house, Joe Cannon reluctantly made his way back along Curzon Street, dreading that the worst would become inevitable. He was never to set eyes upon the Squire again.

Although Cannon had failed in his attempt to bring the Squire back to Newmarket he had succeeded far better than he could realize in reinforcing the doubts in the sick man's mind about the advisability of going to the United States. Even the insensitive companions who forced themselves more closely than ever upon him could see how much he regretted having allowed himself to become involved in the enterprise. He put forward every kind of pretext for not accompanying his fighting men across the Atlantic, but though flashes of the resolution that had made him the greatest Gentleman Rider of the era were still to be seen, his will to resist was broken, and his misgivings were allayed one way or another. All the same, the pugilists, and the others so unashamedly greedy for his money, deemed it prudent to keep him incommunicado until they had set sail from Liverpool and were safely upon the high seas.

Even as the tender took them out of Mersey docks to where the *Majestic*, the great ship of the White Star Line, lay at anchor waiting to take them to the United States, they kept the Squire under anxious surveillance. Knowing the headstrong rashness of which he had been capable in his prime, they feared that his courage might return, and that he would jump overboard to try to swim for shore rather than be forced to go with them.

19 DEATH IN AMERICA

ALTHOUGH crossing the Atlantic in the middle of winter can hardly have been an exhilarating experience, even on board a luxury liner, the voyage revived the Squire's spirits and lifted the feelings of foreboding that had haunted him during his last few weeks in England. Among the party in which he travelled were Charlie Mitchell, Jem Hall, their trainer Billy Woods, Teddy Bayly, his utterly useless secretary, his valet George Monk, ever ready with perfectly meaningless flattery, George McDonald, the bookmaker, and the rest of the fancy. In all, the 4,552-mile journey from London to New Orleans via New York took ten days.

On arrival in New York, Mitchell may have tried to make contact with the hitherto unresponsive Corbett before they went south to New Orleans, where Hall was to fight Fitzsimmons. New Orleans, which lies 107 miles upstream from the mouth of the Mississippi in the state of Louisiana, was a city in which the French influence was still strong in the language, religion and way of life of the descendants of the founders who had named it 'La Nouvelle Orléans' in honour of that Duke of Orleans who had been Regent of France and the greatest rake of his day. In addition to all those people of French descent, New Orleans was inhabited by the creoles of mixed blood, the river boat gamblers and the recently emancipated Negroes, whose music, evolving into jazz, was to do so much to make the city famous throughout the world.

When the Squire arrived in New Orleans in the early March of 1893, the season of carnival, which lasted from the feast of the Epiphany on 6th

January until Mardi Gras, Shrove Tuesday, was in full swing. Parades and processions took place one after another, with the instrumentalists improvising on military marches, in the festooned street throughout the short hours of daylight with the wealthy citizens giving elaborate parties during the longer ones of the night. Still trying to forget the stark and joyless years of reconstruction that followed the Civil War, everybody, everywhere was having fun. In some respects the Squire was as much in his element as he ever could be.

Having booked into the St Charles Hotel, which was being repaired and extended to meet the growing demand for accommodation, the Squire set about spending more of the money earned by the grim toil of his father and grandfather, thereby adding another dimension to that year's carnival. Wherever they went, he and his boon companions broke intermittently into snatches of their recently adopted signature tune, 'Throw 'im down McClusky', a not particularly delicate ditty that offered encouragement to an imaginary Irishman of violent disposition. Making a continual round of the hotels and bars of the city, the Squire bought drinks for anybody who came near him and struck big bets that Jem Hall, whom he was to second himself, would win his fight with Fitzsimmons. Just about everybody wanted to be a friend of the British sportsman who never stopped spending.

Not all the money was spent upon the Americans. Charlie Mitchell saw to that. Urged on by the others, the Squire would do his old trick of throwing a glass of champagne in a bar-tender's face. The man would reach for his six-shooter, whereupon Charlie Mitchell, following carefully rehearsed procedure, vaulted over the counter to disarm him. And the Squire, having been told that only the prompt action of the boxer saved his life, would show his gratitude in the usual substantial manner to the satisfaction of all interested parties, including the bar-tender.

While these charades were being acted out without the Squire becoming involved in the lawlessness of the real gun-fight about which Joe Cannon had been so apprehensive, Meddler, a more imposing individual than ever after his winter's rest, was coming back into strong work on Newmarket heath. Most backers were still putting their money on Isinglass for the Derby, but shrewder and more cautious ones were seeing the possibility of Meddler making enough improvement to beat the McCalmont colt. Early in March, Meddler went particularly well in a gallop up Cambridge Hill on the racecourse side of Newmarket. Among those who watched that work was the London representative of the

Glasgow Herald, the great newspaper of the Squire's home city. Later that day the reporter was shown round Bedford Lodge by Joe Cannon, who again expressed his misgivings that the Squire would never come back from America alive.

Unaware of the serious concern his trainer still felt for his safety, and with no thought of Meddler or the Derby, the Squire embarked upon the duties of second to Jem Hall, full of confidence about the outcome. In the sweating, humid atmosphere of that New Orleans arena, made almost fetid by the breath and cigar smoke of the dense crowd of men packed around the ring, the Squire was tireless in his anxious attendance upon Hall. Although still thin and so weak as to be almost emaciated from his recent attack of pneumonia, he wore no more than a loose vest as he handed bottles of water and packs of ice to his man, hoping ever more frantically that the fortunes of the fight would turn in their favour.

Hungry boxers, according to the old saw, are the best boxers, but it was a long time since the pangs of pain in an empty belly had done anything to inspire Mr James Hall. Brawling in the brothels of the East End or drinking with his patron in the West End had been no way to train for a fight with one of the best boxers in the United States. Making full use of his longer reach, Bob Fitzsimmons soon established an ascendancy, leaving the breathless and belaboured Hall little else to do but paw the air. After the first, second and then the third round, the Squire made despairing and ineffective efforts to revive and put heart into his battered protégé.

As Hall staggered out of his corner in response to the bell that signalled the start of the fourth round, the Squire must have seen that the fight and all his bets were lost. A few seconds later the long arm of Fitzsimmons threw out a punch that put Hall on to the canvas and out for the count.

Following his usual practice in adversity, the Squire sought oblivion and solace in alcohol. With his pride again a lot more badly hurt than his pocket, he set off to get hopelessly drunk on a tour of the city's night-spots with his cronies. Long before dawn it was clear that he had caught a chill, but he still refused to return to the St Charles Hotel to go to bed. Instead, with characteristic recklessness, he insisted on staying out in the cold, early March morning, drinking harder as the sky grew lighter in an attempt to fight off ague and warm his weakening body while his companions tried to cheer him with snatches of 'Throw 'im down McClusky'.

Eventually, he collapsed, and they carried him back to his bed in the St Charles Hotel. When he woke up from a long and drunken sleep, he was suffering from a lot more than the routine hangover, but, though sweating in the agony of the raging fever that had seized his body, he found enough strength to forbid the summoning of a doctor. The services of a trained nurse were, however, obtained.

While the noise of the carpenters hammering away in the adjoining room re-echoed in the frenzied brain of the sick man, Charlie Mitchell sat at his bedside, smoking a huge cigar.

'Wish we were back in good 'ole Lunnon, Squire,' said the boxer.

'Hell's bells, so do I,' groaned the Squire.

'I 'ear as 'ow there's quite a few more blokes down with the fever today,' went on Mitchell.

'Wish we were home,' groaned the Squire, reverting to the previous trend of the conversation.

'They do say,' continued Mitchell with callous indifference to the suffering of his benefactor, 'that once that 'ere malaria gets good 'old of a beggar 'e never gets rid of it. Sorter sticks to 'im and gits in his bloomin' bones, ye know.'

With the carpenter pounding away at his work in the next room, the Squire ignored that cheerless intelligence imparted by his henchman.

'What the hell is that infernal noise?' he asked irritably. 'They've been hammering away for the last bloody half-hour.'

'Well, hye did not want to tell yer, Squire,' said Mitchell, still exhibiting an incredible lack of feeling, 'but the fact is that a poor blighter as was mighty bad with the fever died last night, and they're nailin' him inter a wooden jacket.'

At this point a more sensitive soul in the person of the nurse entered the improvised sick-room. To drown the comforting words she tried to offer her patient, Mitchell burst into yet another chorus of 'Throw 'im down McClusky', in which the Squire, failing though he was, tried to join in a voice that was little above a whisper.

Whether by tact, ruse or downright insistence, the nurse succeeded in calling a doctor. The latter needed no highly specialized medical knowledge to see that Charlie Mitchell's excessively morbid conversation, to say nothing of incessant smoking of cigars, was doing nothing to improve the patient's slender chances of recovery. Accordingly, Mitchell and Hall were persuaded to return to New York on the pretext that they could put in hand arrangements for the former to fight Corbett for the world heavyweight championship. The Squire, they were assured, would follow them as soon as ever he was well enough to do so.

Even the departure of Charlie Mitchell and his cigars, and the intensification of treatment, could do nothing at all to check the rapid deterioration in the Squire's condition. On the afternoon of Friday, 17th March, he became delirious and so violent that he had to be kept under constant surveillance lest he succeeded in doing himself an injury even in his enfeebled state. As a last resort, the doctor called in a second opinion, but his colleague, far from holding out hope, diagnosed the setting in of pneumonia on top of the malarial fever. At eight o'clock on the following morning, Saturday, 18th March 1893, George Alexander Baird, the man born to millions, died in the presence of Teddy Bayly and Monk, young and lonely, and far removed, in every possible sense of the word, from the society that had shunned him as readily as he had outraged it.

All his short life he had run his own race, but the pace he set was far too strong to give him any chance of getting the distance. The fate spared him was that the money did not run out, despite his monumental extravagance.

A few hours after the Squire had died, Charlie Mitchell and Jem Hall arrived in New York by the train that pulled into Grand Central Station at five to four. Mitchell's intention to challenge Corbett for the championship was already public knowledge, and the press were eager to know whether the death of his backer would cause the cancellation of the project. Everybody, including the American newspapermen, seemed to know that there was not the slightest chance of the Squire's family or executors honouring his commitments. To these questions Mitchell had a complete answer. The money had been a gift to him with which to back himself. 'Mr Baird put up 10,000 dollars,' he said as cockily as ever, 'on the understanding that hye should have it all if hye won. That's the way the Squire always backed 'is men.'

Asked by reporters about the condition of the Squire when he last saw him, Mitchell replied, 'When hye left New Horleans the Squire was in bed,' adding with somewhat naïve candour, 'His doctor advised me to leave, saying he would recover more quickly!' Finally Mitchell told his interviewers, 'Before hye left hye said if they could get the Squire well enough to catch Wednesday's boat from New York hye would give them 1,000 dollars.' The remark said less for Mitchell's generosity, as he would, as usual, have been using his patron's own money, than it did for his total incomprehension of the gravity of the Squire's illness.

Having satisfied the curiosity of the reporters, Mitchell wired instructions to New Orleans that the body of the Squire should be embalmed and sent to New York so that it could be taken back to England aboard the *Majestic*. He then set about making his last frantic, fruitless efforts to secure a fight with Corbett at some later date.

Unlike Mitchell, who had performed the duties of drinking companion, nursemaid, bodyguard and prison understudy to perfection, Teddy Bayly had been of minimal use to the Squire during his lifetime and proved of even less use after his death. On receiving instructions from Mitchell, the secretary found himself at a complete loss as to how to arrange for the embalming of the body. Had it not been for the good offices of the British Consul, the final irony in the story of the Squire would have been his burial in an unmarked pauper's grave on the other side of the world. Thanks to that official, however, the coffin reached New York in time for the sailing of the *Majestic* on the Wednesday.

On reaching Liverpool, the body of the Squire was taken home to be laid beside that of his father in the family vault in the little churchyard at Stichil. Close by was the great house in which he had been so sadly ill-prepared for a world that held such immeasurable promise.

The life of George Alexander Baird could be said to have been a continual illustration of the truth of the divine saying that it is easier for a camel to pass through an eye of a needle that it is for a rich man to enter the kingdom of heaven. In his case, the burden of his great material possessions was made harder to bear by what he lacked in the abstract. Not only was he deprived of firm guidance, so essential to one of his character and circumstances, by the death of his father in childhood, but, unlike his cousin Edward Baird, who had been left fatherless at a still earlier age, he had no older brothers to set him an example and help in the moulding of his personality. Moreover, in complete contrast to Edward Baird, he was without either a strong intellect or any deep resources of moral character.

Yet, for all that narrow-minded and self-righteous critics have said or written about him, George Baird cannot be dismissed as a weak and bad man by any stretch of the imagination. While it is true that he could have been a great deal more selective in the recipients of his charity, he deserves credit for having had that rare thing, a kind heart. His saving of the life of his one-time friend Jimmy Shaw by defraying the huge medical costs involved was just one example of many acts of generosity for which there was not the ghost of ulterior motive. It is, perhaps, arguable that he was killed by his own kindness. Had he not been unduly anxious to please those whom he so mistakenly thought wished to please him, he might never have been steered along the course that led to his death.

The great contradiction in an apparently uncomplicated character was that, whereas he was capable of great generosity, he could, and often did, behave like a bully with his hired prize-fighters on hand to protect him from his just deserts. To some extent, this unattractive trait can be attributed to the fashion in humour during the late Victorian era. The practical joke was very much in vogue, and a boisterous, unsophisticated schoolboy sense of humour was best appealed to by the occasioning of physical discomfiture. One of the favourite party tricks of the Prince of Wales was to pour brandy over the solemn Yorkshire landowner, Christopher Sykes, just to hear him intone the words, 'As your Royal Highness pleases.' To some extent, some of the most objectionable and unseemly behaviour of the Squire can be ascribed to his carrying a trend to extremes.

The other element of contradiction in his character lay in the contrast between the inflexible determination that so much impressed Bob Armstrong and others at the height of his riding career, and the ease with which he could be led. Having set his heart upon doing something, George Baird showed all the strength of character of his father, uncles and grandfather. No man of a weak or irresolute turn of mind could have endured the physical privations that he did in order to be able to ride at less than 10 stone. Nor could such a man have had the dedication and concentration to have developed a technique which, even his detractors agreed, was little inferior to that of any of the best of the professional jockeys. Few men or women, no matter how ample the means at their disposal, leave this world with the satisfaction of having been able to do anything superlatively well. The Squire had that satisfaction. He was a superlatively good amateur jockey by the standards of any age. For that alone he was remarkable. Even allowing for his having had the wealth to mount himself in almost any race for which he could do the weight, his achievement in riding more than sixty winners in a single season under Jockey Club rules remains truly memorable.

Unfortunately, though he had the will-power that enabled him to realize his ambition to be far and away the most successful Gentleman Rider in the country, he was altogether without the moral strength to resist the multitude of temptations that beset him. Added to this, he was such a deplorable judge of character as to be the ideal victim for all but the most implausible swindlers.

Having been hopelessly spoilt and pampered by his mother in late childhood, he was neither amenable to discipline nor able to form friendships with other boys during the short time that he was at Eton. After that rebuff by contemporaries of his own wealth and background on his first venture from home, he felt himself cut off from all of them, save those that shared his passion for race riding, for the rest of his life. That sense of being ostracized and discriminated against was heightened by his feeling that he had been unfairly warned off the Turf by men who were not only judge and jury in their own cause but ill-disposed towards him from the outset. In consequence, he turned to the workshy young men, the gamblers, confidence tricksters and ladies of varying degrees of virtue for his friends. The only thing that all those people had in common was a vested interest in seeing that he never grew out of the folly of late adolescence and put his immense fortune to good use. In defence of that ignoble interest, they destroyed him.

POSTSCRIPT

WHEN Lillie Langtry received news of the death of the Squire, she was enjoying an early spring cruise in the Mediterranean on board the *Whyte Lady*, still irreverently known as the 'Black Eye'. Whatever grief she may have felt at the premature passing of her former paramour quickly gave way to an urgent desire to ascertain how much he had left her as the last token of his very far from tender love. On putting in to the nearest port, which was Nice, she was frustrated by finding all trains to the north fully booked for the rest of the day, but an English gentleman, anxious to help a lady apparently in deep distress, gave up his seat on the Rapide to her.

On arrival in London, she went straight to the Conduit Street office of the Squire's solicitor, Walter Lumley, in company with her own solicitor, Sir George Lewis, to make inquiries about the disposition of the Squire's estate. In a cold, unfriendly voice, Lumley informed her that everything had been left to the family. No strangers were mentioned.

Flabbergasted as she recalled how the Squire had pledged his eternal love for her, and how he had promised that all that he possessed would one day be hers, and forgetting the state of intoxication in which such undertakings had been given, she demanded to see the will and codicils. Still impassive and unsympathetic, the lawyer informed her that there was no necessity for her to see them. No strangers were mentioned.

Had he been of a mind to do so, Walter Lumley could have told her that, despite all the sorrow and disappointment the Squire had caused his mother, his devotion to her had never diminished. For all the loyalty he had shown to his worthless associates, his last loyalty of all had been to the family from which he had estranged himself for so long. By his will, dated 14th November 1891, he had left everything in trust for his mother for life, with the capital to be divided equally among such of the children of his first cousins as should survive her.

He then had added a codicil about a fortnight later, directing that the ultimate beneficiaries should be those children of his first cousins, his first cousins once removed, who should survive both his mother and himself. Finally, contrary to the sincerest hopes of Lillie Langtry, Charlie Mitchell and a good few more of either ilk, a second codicil, signed when Walter Lumley had come to the Curzon Street house in early February, had made even less material difference to the original will than the first. All the second codicil did was to direct that the property in land included all that which he owned in Scotland, thereby ensuring that no confusion arose through Scottish law being different from English, and 'in order that no doubt or [sic] dispute should arise', it made the powers of his trustees transferable to their heirs and assigns. From first to last there was no mention of any strangers, even though the Squire had been unable to single out any one of his relatives for a personal memento, a special legacy or even to be mentioned individually, save the mother on whom he had doted for thirty-one years.

The only other trustee of the will besides Walter Lumley was Ernest de Witt, a barrister. On 6th May 1893, they received probate from the High Court, the Squire's estate having been assessed at £846,051 12s. 11d. The fact of the deceased sportsman having left almost a million pounds after ten years of incessant expenditure and casual distribution of gifts, in cash and kind, to almost anyone out for a touch, was a cause of much astonishment. Almost equally surprising, to most people's way of thinking, was that his hangers-on and mistresses did not get a penny piece between them.

Under the terms of his will, the executors were empowered to dispose of any of the assets left by the Squire in order to reinvest the proceeds. Among the assets those two solemn, legal gentlemen considered entirely superfluous to the requirement of the trust they administered were, of course, the racing establishments. The leases of Bedford Lodge and Whittington Old Hall were surrendered as soon as possible, and Moulton Paddocks was sold to Sir Ernest Cassel, the financier friend of the Prince of Wales. Finally, all the horses, or, rather, those officially registered as the property of the Squire, were put up for sale by Messrs Tattersalls.

The dispersal sale of the Squire's string and stud took place in two stages. Thirty older horses, fourteen two-year-olds and four yearlings were offered at Tattersalls first July sale, on 26th June 1893, while the stallions, broodmares, foals and the rest of the yearlings were retained for another year. Inevitably Meddler was the centre of attention at the first sale, despite his no longer being qualified to meet Isinglass in the St Leger or to fulfil engagements made for him in any of the other important races that had already closed. As the rules of racing stood until Edgar Wallace, the writer, brought a friendly case against the Jockey Club thirty-four years later, in 1927, all engagements made for a horse automatically became void on the death of its nominator.

Consequently Meddler had already missed the Two Thousand Guineas and the Derby. Nevertheless Meddler still had immense value as the unbeaten son of a Derby winner and an Oaks winner, and a group of English owners formed a syndicate with a view to preventing him from being sold abroad. When the syndicate's agent went to the maximum with a bid of 14,000 guineas, however, he was immediately capped by Mr Forbes, acting in American interests, with one of 14,500 guineas.

Meddler proved a serious loss to the British Turf as he got a great many winners in the United States, where he was twice leading sire. Subsequently he was sold for a sum in the region of his original price to Mr Clarence Mackay, who sent him to France. There he died at the Haras de Frensay-le-Buffard in Normandy in 1916. Before leaving the United States, he had sired Armenis, who became dam of the 1914 Derby winner Durbar II.

The name of Meddler has not disappeared from British racing. The Kentford Stud, at which he was bred by the Squire, has been renamed the Meddler Stud and is now managed by its owner, Mr W. B. Leach.

None of the other horses in the first draft made anything like as much as Meddler. The next highest price was the 1,400 guineas fetched by the eight-year-old mare, Lady Rosebery, who had won the Liverpool Autumn Cup in 1888 and 1890, finished third in it in 1891 and 1892 and fourth in 1889. She was bought by Lillie Langtry, for whom she won the Jockey Club Cup in the autumn. Lillie also paid 730 guineas for the three-year-old Studley Royal, who was successful at Yarmouth and Windsor soon afterwards. The aggregate made by the forty lots in the first draft was 36,230 guineas.

The second draft of the Squire's horses was offered by Tattersalls at

Newmarket on Monday, 2nd July 1894. This consisted of Merry Hampton, Juggler and three stallions of no significance, nine broodmares with their foals, four other broodmares and six yearlings. Rather surprisingly, Juggler fetched more than Merry Hampton, being bought by Mr R. Stubbings, of Newmarket's Park Paddocks stud, for 1,750 guineas, while the Derby winner went to George Barrett, the fashionable jockey, for 1,550 guineas. Merry Hampton's only claim to fame as a stallion is as the sire of Merry Token. She was the mother of Mahubah, who threw the great American horse Man O'War, winner of the Preakness Stakes, the Belmont Stakes and eighteen of his other nineteen races.

Most expensive of the broodmares was, predictably enough, Busybody, who was bought for 3,500 guineas by Sir John Blundell Maple for his Childwick Bury Stud. Sir John also bought the second most expensive of the broodmares by paying 1,750 guineas for Superba. Busybody's foal by St Gatien, the full sister to Meddler, was bought by Sir Hamar Bass, the brewer, for 930 guineas, while Jimmy Waugh bought both Juggler's dam Enchantress and her colt foal by Merry Hampton for 300 guineas and 520 guineas respectively. The six yearlings made no more than 670 guineas between them, the Squire's old adversary in the selling plate game, Captain Machell, paying 110 guineas for the brown colt already named Mitre. As he was by Merry Hampton, this colt must have been named after the Mitre, the old coaching inn near Hampton Court, in which the Squire would have tippled after racing at Hurst Park.

In all, the thirty-two horses in the second draft fetched 13,886 guineas. This brought the total sum made by the Squire's bloodstock to 52,621 guineas. That sum would have been rather higher had the trustees had their way. Being unable to find a deed of gift relating to Milford among the morass of papers that the Squire had left strewn around the Curzon Street house and Bedford Lodge, they demanded that Lillie Langtry should return the colt to the estate. Now that he was no longer eligible for the Derby, Lillie bitterly regretted not accepting the 20,000 guineas that she had been offered for him after the Coventry Stakes, but she had no intention whatever of acceding to the request of the trustees, and thanks to the deft intervention of Sir George Lewis, was able to refuse it out of hand. This left Messrs Lumley and de Witt more highly incensed than ever at the thought of the *Whyte Lady* and all the other presents, to say nothing of the money, that she had had from the Squire to the immense detriment of the family whose interests they represented. For her part, having recovered from the sheer amazement it had caused her, Lillie was still absolutely livid at being left out of the Squire's will. To have been made to surrender Milford would have been to have had the last grain of salt rubbed in a festering wound. In due course, Milford won her ten more races before being retired to the Kentford Stud at a fee of 10 guineas at the end of his seven-year-old days. Within three years of the death of the Squire, Lillie had her own string trained privately by Fred Webb in the Ethelreda House stable on the road between Newmarket and Exning.

In the autumn of 1896, William Allison, the journalist who had been among the most persistent critics of the Squire, told her that the Australian four-year-old Merman was for sale and likely to win a good race over a distance of ground. Lillie agreed to pay 1,600 guineas for him, and on 13th October 1897, her forty-fourth birthday, he won the Cesarewitch, carrying 7 stone 5 pounds. Forty-eight hours later, Edward Langtry, the man cuckolded by the Prince of Wales, the Squire and others of the most illustrious and infamous in the land, died, weak and feckless to the last, in a nursing home in Cheshire.

Merman, who had legs like steel, stayed in training until he was an eight-year-old in 1900. That year he won the Gold Cup, having brought off the double in the Goodwood Cup and the Goodwood Plate the previous one. He was retired to the Cobham stud, managed by William Allison, in Surrey, but was not a success as a stallion and sold to Germany for 500 guineas in 1908.

Two years after the death of Edward Langtry, Lillie married the handsome, vapid Hugo de Bathe, seventeen years her junior and heir to a baronetcy, while continuing with her career as an actress. In 1908, she won another Cesarewitch when Yentoi, trained by twenty-four-year-old Fred Darling, brought off a big gamble for the Beckhampton stable. Although the rules of racing still allowed the use of assumed names, Yentoi ran as the property of Lady de Bathe.

Lillie, once the woman the Squire had fondled in public, was just turned fifty-five when Yentoi won the Cesarewitch. She lived more than another twenty years, dying in Monaco on 12th February 1929.

Three of the men with whom the Squire had been closely associated on the Turf, the Marquess of Ailesbury, Bob Peck and Jack Watts, survived him by less than a decade. Lord Ailesbury, the Billy Stomachache of jollier days, paid the price of his own profligacy by dying with no known worthwhile achievement to his name at the age of thirty-one in 1894. Bob Peck, having retired from training prematurely, was already in indifferent health when he undertook the impossible, if highly remunerative, task of managing the unmanageable at Bedford Lodge. He was only fifty-four when he died at Scarborough in August 1899.

Jack Watts, who won the first of his four Derbys on Merry Hampton, had to waste drastically during the last years that he was riding, and had only just turned to training when he collapsed at Sandown Park in 1902. He was too ill to be moved, and died at the age of forty-one ten days later. His son and his grandson, both his namesakes, trained with considerable success, as does his great-grandson, Bill Watts, at Richmond today.

As if to compensate them for the tribulations involved in handling the Squire's horses and coping with his friends, providence endowed his private trainers with longevity. All three were over eighty when they died.

Martin Gurry trained for twenty-seven years in the Abington Place stable he built with the money that the Squire had to pay him. He gained his second classic success with Sir James Miller's La Sagesse in the Oaks of 1895, retired in 1917 and died in 1923. In recent years, Abington Place, the most enduring memorial to the Squire, has been the quarters of former champion jockey Harry Wragg, who has made it one of the most successful stables in Europe.

On leaving Bedford Lodge, Charlie Morton was successively private trainer to three more owners who were every bit as outrageously extraordinary as the Squire in their different ways. The first was Colonel John North, who never learned a thing about horses or racing. He had made a fortune out of nitrates in Chile and had the Chetwynd House (now Machell Place) stable at Newmarket. After him, Charlie Morton went to the discredited American politician 'Boss' Croker for a short while, and then to Bob Siever, for whom he trained Sceptre as a two-year-old. Finally, in 1902, he entered upon calmer waters by becoming private trainer to the diamond millionaire, Mr J. B. Joel, with whom he enjoyed a highly successful association based on mutual trust for twenty-two years. For Mr Joel he won the Derby with Sunstar (1911) and Humorist (1921) as well as nine other classics. Charlie Morton retired in 1921 and died in a nursing home in Brighton in February 1936.

After the dispersal of the Squire's horses, Joe Cannon finally opened a public stable at Lordship Farm, Newmarket, now a stud. He became a specialist at winning the Manchester November Handicap, the big betting race that was traditionally run on the last day of the season until the closing of the Castle Irwell course in 1963. He won it with Lexicon in

1900, and again with The Valet (1910), Dalmatian (1913) and Planted (1917). He also won the Lincolnshire with Mercutio (1911), the Royal Hunt Cup with Csardas (1904) and the Cambridgeshire with Adam Bede (1911).

On retiring in 1919, Joe Cannon handed the Lordship Farm stable to his son, J. H. S. Cannon. As the latter had inherited his father's love of the ring, and had no small aptitude with the gloves, he was never known as anything but 'Boxer' Cannon, a nickname that served as an indirect reminder of the way in which his father and the Squire had come to know each other. Joe Cannon, who was eighty-three when he died in 1933, was also the father of Noel Cannon. While private trainer to Mr J. V. Rank at Druids Lodge, Noel Cannon won many important races, including the St Leger in 1938 with Scottish Union.

Tom Cannon, who rode and trained Busybody for the Squire, was seventy-one when he died in 1917. He gave up training in 1892 and later bought the Grosvenor Arms at Stockbridge, where he lived in some comfort while a manager ran the business of the inn during his latter years. In the wooden panelling of the dining room of the Grosvenor Arms are carved representations on many of the great horses Tom Cannon rode. Unfortunately, Busybody is not among them.

Charlie Morbey was another to survive four score years, as he was eighty-two when he died in November 1938. He took care to see that he made a great deal of money out of managing the racing interests of the Squire, for some time after whose death he was a comparatively wealthy man. He owned a number of horses, which he ran in the name of 'Mr Ellis', for reasons best known to himself, including Red Eyes, who dead-heated with Cypria in the Cesarewitch. Eventually, though, his luck turned and he lost a lot of money betting so that he had to sell much of his property. Towards the end of his life, he was much reduced in circumstances, his old age having been further saddened by the death of his eldest son, Captain C. F. W. Morbey, in action in 1917.

The valet George Monk also made sure he put enough away for a rainy day while in the service of the Squire. Shortly after the death of his employer, Mr Monk blossomed forth as the landlord of the Horse and Groom at Streatham.

Teddy Bayly, who acted as the Squire's secretary on that fatal visit to the United States, took to innkeeping in a rather more elevated sphere than Monk. For many years he was the landlord of the Queen's Hotel, Leicester Square. He was also at the English Hotel, Boulougne, for a while, and just before the outbreak of the First World War, he was keeping the Nayland Rock Hotel at Margate. He was the brother-in-law of Harry Preston, who had the Royal York Hotel at Brighton.

Of the two cousins against whom the Squire had raced, Douglas Baird did not survive him by many years. He was still in his early fifties when he died in the winter of 1908–9.

Edward Baird, a contrast to his cousin in lifespan as in all else, survived to be over ninety in the second half of the present century. Over the years Ned Baird, the sporting young soldier-rider of the Squire's day, matured into a highly competent general officer. In addition, he was a figure of considerable importance on the Turf, both as an owner and as an administrator.

Shortly before his marriage to Millicent, daughter of General Sir Stanley Clarke, in 1893, Edward bought the Exning House estate a mile or two to the north of Newmarket. Having almost rebuilt the mansion and modernized the imposing stableyard, he engaged Harry Enoch as private trainer to himself, his brother Douglas, Lord Penrhyn and a few other friends.

Captain Baird, as he was at the time, was elected to the Jockey Club in 1894, the year after the death of the Squire. In 1904, he began a three-year term as steward, automatically becoming senior steward in 1906, and the following year saw his colours carried to success in the St Leger by Woolwinder.

In 1891, he had bought a yearling filly by Springfield out of Queen of the Hills from John Porter. Subsequently named Queen of the Spring, she never won a race but became the dam of several winners, including St Windeline (by St Simon) who was second to Sceptre in the One Thousand Guineas. St Windeline's first mate on being retired to stud was Douglas Baird's 1892 Goodwood Cup winner Martagon. To him she bred Woolwinder, who was trained by Enoch at Exning.

In 1900, Edward Baird, then holding the rank of major, went to South Africa to serve with the Imperial Yeomanry in the Boer War. From 1901 to 1906, he was a lieutenant-colonel commanding the Suffolk Hussars, and was later promoted brigadier-general.

The almost unbelievable opulence of Edwardian England had long disappeared when General Baird died at the great age of ninety-two at his home at Duns, Berwickshire, in August 1956. For many years he had been the doyen of the Jockey Club, something the Squire would never have been had he lived to be a hundred.

BIBLIOGRAPHY

ACTON, C. R., *Silk and Spur* (n.d.).

ALLISON, WIlliam, *Memories of Men and Horses* (1922).

ANDRE, Sam, and FLEISCHER, Nat, *A Pictorial History of Boxing* (1975).

BLUNT, Bruce, *Arthur Yates* (1924).

BOOTH, J. B., *Old Pink 'Un Days* (1926).

CHALMERS, Patrick R., *Racing in England* (1939).

DEY, Thomas Henry, *Leaves from a Bookmaker's Book* (n.d.).

FAIRFAX-BLAKEBOROUGH, J., *Paddock Personalities* (1938).

LAMBTON, Hon. George, *Men and Horses I Have Known* (1924).

MORTIMER, Roger, *The History of the Derby Stakes* (1973).

MORTON, Charles, *My Sixty Years on the Turf* (n.d.).

NEVILL, Ralph, *The Sport of Kings* (1926).

NEVILL, Ralph, *The Gay Victorians* (1930).

RODRIGO, Robert, *The Racing Game* (1958).

SCOTT, Alexander, *Turf Memories of Sixty Years* (n.d.).

SILTZER, Frank, *Newmarket* (1923).

SUTHERLAND, Douglas, *The Yellow Earl* (1965).

VOIGHT, Charles Adolph, *Famous Gentleman Riders* (1925).

WELCOME, John, *Fred Archer, His Life and Times* (1967).

WELCOME, John, *Neck or Nothing* (1970).

Also consulted, various issues of:

Sporting Chronicle
Glasgow Herald
Bloodstock Breeders Review
Racing Calendar
General Stud Book
Vanity Fair

GENERAL INDEX

INDEX OF RACEHORSE NAMES